THE
RAINFORESTS
A CELEBRATION

LOBSTER CLAW *(HELICONIA WAGNERIANA)*
(Gerry Ellis/Ellis Wildlife Collection)

THE
RAINFORESTS
A CELEBRATION

COMPILED BY THE LIVING EARTH FOUNDATION
EDITED BY LISA SILCOCK

FOREWORD BY H.R.H. THE PRINCE OF WALES

OPPOSITE: BUTTRESS ROOTS IN RAINFOREST, COSTA RICA
(Michael & Patricia Fogden)

CRESSET
PRESS

THE LIVING EARTH FOUNDATION is a registered UK environmental charity with education as the main focus of its work. Royalties from this book will go to a project in Cameroon, West Africa, whose aim is to work through schools to enable local communities to understand and value their precious environment and to manage their resources for the future. This is the first of what Living Earth intends will be a series of effective and innovative projects in tropical rainforest countries.

FOREWORD

To walk in a tropical rainforest, as I was lucky enough to do on a recent visit to South America, is an intriguing experience. It is impossible not to feel awed by the beauty of the forest, by its immensity, by the sense of a history spanning millions of years. Giant trees stretch skywards, lifting their leaves a hundred feet or more to the light, their shallow roots supported by writhing buttresses. The air is moist, rich with the smell of rotting leaves.

Animals are hard to see in the dense forest vegetation, although you hear a veritable cacophony of hidden insects and birds. For me, one of the most memorable features was the number of stunningly beautiful butterflies which flitted across my path. Sounds are a clue to the rainforest, which is quite literally seething with life: worldwide, rainforests contain over half the species on earth.

But tropical rainforests are being destroyed at horrifying rates and on a scale that threatens us all. Species of plants are becoming extinct even before their potential benefits are known. When the rainforests go, water and soil are ruined, and the prospects for development and productive use of the land disappear. On a world scale, the possible effect on climatic stability could affect us all.

If only more people understood how economic prospects and potential for development are tied into the care and protection of natural resources, consumers and decision-makers might take different priorities when it comes to rainforests. There is no easy solution, but part of the answer must lie in education. Without education, efforts to protect the environment – rainforest or otherwise – are unlikely to gain the support necessary to enable them to succeed.

The Rainforests: A Celebration, besides being a celebration of these extraordinary ecosystems, also serves to build on the existing awareness and produce a deeper understanding of the role tropical rainforests play in the natural balance of our planet. It shows exactly what we stand to lose if this destruction continues and demonstrates why we must not allow this to happen. But the only way of preventing the destruction is if the developed world understands the costs involved. The developing countries have to be given assistance to achieve these aims.

In buying this book you also contribute directly to the future of rainforests. The Living Earth Foundation works for environmental education in Britain and elsewhere. The royalties from this book will go to support their project in Cameroon, which teaches schoolchildren living in and around rainforests about their environment. These children will form a new generation: one which, we hope, will know how to protect and manage its irreplaceable heritage.

LIST OF CONTRIBUTORS

PROFESSOR GHILLEAN T. PRANCE is Director of the Royal Botanic Gardens, Kew. He was President of the Association of Tropical Botany (USA) in 1979/80 and of the American Society of Plant Taxonomists in 1984/5. He is currently President of the Systematics Association.

DR JULIAN CALDECOTT is a rainforest ecologist who has been involved in many projects concerning wildlife and forest conservation throughout South-East Asia. He is currently managing a major new national park in Nigeria.

DR TOM LOVEJOY, a tropical and conservation biologist, has worked in the Amazon forest of Brazil since 1965. From 1973 to 1987 he directed the programme of the World Wildlife Fund (US). In 1987 he was appointed Assistant Secretary for External Affairs at the Smithsonian Institution.

P. MICK RICHARDSON is currently a biochemical systematist at the New York Botanical Garden. He is author of a volume on hallucinogenic angiosperms and is writing a book on the evolution and ecology of toxic plants.

DR CAROLINE PANNELL holds a teaching post in the Department of Plant Sciences at the University of Oxford.

JONATHAN KINGDON is an evolutionary biologist, artist and author of numerous books and papers on mammals and visual communication in animals. He is now based in the Department of Zoology at the University of Oxford.

ANDREW MITCHELL is an author and zoologist who pioneered the use of lightweight aerial walkways to study the rainforest canopy. He is currently Marketing Director of Earthwatch.

PROFESSOR DAVID BELLAMY, botanist, writer and broadcaster was Senior Lecturer in botany at Durham University until 1982 when he founded the Conservation Foundation.

ROBIN HANBURY-TENISON is President of Survival International. In 1977-8, as one of Britain's leading explorers and travellers, he led 140 scientists to Borneo on the biggest expedition ever mounted by the Royal Geographical Society, which sparked off international concern for tropical rainforests.

ROGER HAMMOND is the Founder Director and Chief Executive of Living Earth.

LISA SILCOCK was assistant producer of the BAFTA Award winning film for Channel 4, *Baka – People of the Rainforest*. To make the film she lived with the Baka Pygmies in Cameroon, West Africa, for two years, learning to speak the language fluently. She is a freelance writer.

CONTENTS

INTRODUCTION
PROFESSOR GHILLEAN T. PRANCE

THIS BOOK IS CALLED **THE RAINFORESTS: A CELEBRATION.** A strange title, perhaps, at a time when the forests' very existence is threatened. What is there to celebrate, after all? The media bombard us daily with the appalling facts and consequences of rainforest destruction; public concern has risen to unprecedented levels; even politicians are embracing the issues.

The loss of the world's tropical rainforests is undoubtedly one of the most serious crises we face today. But while many of us can now quote horrifying statistics (an area the size of Britain burned every year; a hundred or more species becoming extinct every day), we have only the haziest picture of what the rainforests are and why they are so important. We understand the destruction; not what is actually being destroyed.

Once, rainforest covered the tropics to form an almost continuous girdle around the earth, broken only by the sea and odd areas of land whose climate was unsuitable. There are three major rainforest regions: South and Central America, which holds nearly three-fifths of the world's total; South East Asia, and West and Central Africa. Smaller patches occur in Australasia, the Far East and the Indian sub-continent, as well as on scattered islands throughout the tropics. But today, largely

BASILISK WAITING TO AMBUSH PASSING PREY IN TROPICAL RAINFOREST, COSTA RICA

(Ken Preston-Mafham/Premaphotos)

CHAPTER ONE

THE RAINFOREST – AN OVERVIEW
DR JULIAN CALDECOTT

The rainforest is a living miracle of complexity, formed by more than half the species of animals and plants on earth – possibly many more. Although it supports millions of people directly, it and its products are also inextricably woven into our own lives, far away from the tropics. But as most of us are now aware, rainforests everywhere are being decimated, and with them, the life they support. There is no straightforward solution to this great threat; but though our knowledge of this most sophisticated of ecosystems is still very incomplete, the more we do understand of its complexity and fragility, the more we appreciate the imperative of protecting it. What, then, makes it so extraordinary; why must it be saved? What is this community of living things which we call rainforest?

THE TROPICAL RAINFORESTS OF THE WORLD ARE ancient, complex ecosystems, teeming with diverse life forms. Here, there are soaring trees, their trunks often buttressed; a lofty canopy of branches and leaves, with deep shade below; climbing lianas and palms; plants growing on other plants; a rather bare forest floor, with lumpy roots writhing across it, a dusting of fallen leaves, and scattered ferns and seedlings. Butterflies dance in rare shafts of sunlight from above, birds make exotic noises, and insects sizzle and click.

This restless background is often overlaid by the rattling thunder of rain on distant leaves, and the dripping of water as it drains out of the canopy. The combination of warmth and rain makes the air of the forest very humid, often saturated with water vapour. Mists shroud the trees as sun succeeds storm,

---

1 **SIERRA PALM FOREST, EL YUNQUE, PUERTO RICO**
(Gerry Ellis/Ellis Wildlife Collection)

BETWEEN THE TROPICS OF CANCER AND CAPRICORN, FROM QUEENSLAND AND BORNEO TO BIAFRA AND YUCATAN OR AMAZONIA, WHERE THE TEMPERATURE IS HIGH AND CONSTANT AND THE ANNUAL RAINFALL IS MORE THAN 250MM/100IN, A DISTINCT TYPE OF FOREST GROWS. THESE ARE THE TROPICAL RAINFORESTS OF THE WORLD: ANCIENT, COMPLEX ECOSYSTEMS, TEEMING WITH DIVERSE LIFE FORMS, SHELTERING MORE THAN HALF THE SPECIES OF PLANTS AND ANIMALS ON EARTH – SOME BELIEVE MANY MORE. THEY COVER AN AREA ROUGHLY THE SIZE OF THE US – THREE-FIFTHS OF THIS IS IN CENTRAL AND SOUTH AMERICA. THEY ARE THE MOST THREATENED, IRREPLACEABLE AND VALUABLE ENVIRONMENTS IN THE WORLD.

rising up to form heavy clouds which pour out rain in their turn.

High temperatures and rainfall, more or less constant throughout the year, combine to produce the warm steamy atmosphere common to all the world's tropical rainforests, from Queensland to the Amazon basin. In these hothouse conditions, protected from cold and drought, plants and animals flourish in dazzling and as yet incalculable variety.

Paradoxically, one of the elements on which this teeming life depends also poses its greatest natural threat, and it is everywhere: dripping, trickling, prying into every crevice, water if left to its own devices would leach away all the forest's scarce and precious nutrients. Every organism in the forest is adapted to this perpetual battle against the insidious power of water. As a result, it has been estimated that only about one per cent of its total nutrients is eventually washed away by the rain.

Over the years, other adaptations have taken place; the longer a rainforest exists, the more intimate become the relationships between the multitudinous organisms of which it is composed. Over time, species adapt to one another: animals to plants, plants to animals, animals to animals, and plants to plants, each lineage refining its ecological 'niche' from generation to generation. This means that the requirements a species has for survival, and the ways in which it fulfils these needs, become more and more distinct over time. Animals and plants thus become increasingly successful survivors, ever more efficient exploiters or avoiders of exploitation. The tendency is for animals to get better and better at eating fewer and fewer things, for prey to protect themselves more and more rigorously, for plants to grow in increasingly special situations, and for particular species to make arrangements of mutual benefit with others - food and shelter, for example, exchanged for help in defence.

As species become more specialized, they leave room for others, and so give rise to new species with narrower ecological niches. As this occurs, the collective mass of species present in the environment becomes increasingly efficient at gathering, using and re-using essential nutrients. Members of species with very narrow ecological requirements do tend to be scarce, however. The reason for this is that they can only make use of resources (such as nutrients) which are in the particular form that they are adapted to exploit, and any such specific form will not be common; in addition, only a limited quantity of resources in any form is available in the forest at any one time. The outcome of all this is that in rainforests there are very many (mostly rare) species, living in very many curious and interdependent ways.

No other habitat on earth contains such a profusion or weight of plant life per hectare. Under the tropical sun, moreover, everything grows at astonishing speed. The rainforest produces new vegetable tissues faster than any other community on land. But death, too, is ever-present. A smell of decay hangs in the air and underfoot is a thin layer of debris. The forest's dynamism is fuelled by the speed of decay in the hot, damp, atmosphere, which acts as an incubator for scavenging and digesting organisms, and by the powerful flow of nutrient-carrying water from the ground to the canopy, drawn by the suction of evaporation from its myriad leaves. The rainforest is thus in dynamic balance, at a hectic rate of turnover.

It is the bright light of the tropical sun which powers the rainforest. Using solar energy, plants manufacture simple sugars from carbon dioxide in the atmosphere and from water, by the chemical process of photosynthesis. These sugars are the building-blocks of molecules which make up plants' cell walls and woody substance. Furthermore, they can be broken down as needed to provide energy and atoms for use in the complex biochemistry of life. They are used first by the plant that made them and subsequently, in one form or another, by organisms able to take them from the plant, or to retrieve them from its remains.

The structure of the rainforest is dictated by one overriding factor: almost all light is captured by the forest's canopy, casting the interior into deep shade. If a plant is to support itself by photosynthesis, it must therefore either be able to manage in semi-darkness, or it must somehow get its leaves into the canopy. A few plants are adapted to the shade of the rainforest floor, but they make up only a tiny portion of the forest's total flora. They include many ferns, the begonias, broad-leaved grasses and sedges, and gingers. More often to be seen in this twilight zone are small palms, bushes, seedlings and saplings, most of them destined one day, with luck, to reach the canopy as trees or lianas.

The rainforest is essentially a gallery whose monumental structure is made up of trees: their trunks provide its lower levels with a vertical framework, while the higher branches form a latticework roof. The tallest trees may be as much as sixty metres (200 feet) high, their trunks five metres (16 feet) in diameter near the ground, and often braced by woody buttresses like massive twisted fins. Trees of this size, known as 'emergents' are in a minority, however, and their crowns usually tower over those of their neighbours. Below them, the forest canopy becomes more continuous, the crowns of most adult trees standing shoulder to shoulder in a deep layer fifteen to forty-five metres (50-150 feet) above the forest floor.

This main level of the canopy is translucent, the light declining steadily in intensity as it filters through the leaves. This mass of vegetation offers opportunities for life to plants adapted to different and very specific degrees of illumination and, since the air within the forest is wetter than that outside, of moisture. Different tree species slot their adult crowns into the canopy at different heights depending on their physiological needs. Clinging to their branches and leaves, or to each other, are lesser plants which share their preferences – lichens and mosses, ferns and orchids in great and varied profusion. Interwoven within and draped across the canopy are the stems and foliage of climbing palms and lianas, which help to bind the forest into a continuous physical structure, and which often form a large part of the canopy itself.

In this intimidatingly diverse and dynamic environment, most of the action is hidden from view. Scientific documentation of the evolutionary relationships among the millions of rainforest species has only just begun, and many of the subtleties are only now starting to be explored. These include, for example, the ways in which 'arms races' between predators and their prey, herbivores and the plants they eat, can lead to chemical and behavioural defences of amazing power and complexity. They also include ways in which species manipulate others to achieve their own reproductive ends through pollination or seed dispersal.

But we are rapidly losing the chances of furthering this knowledge, and the wisdom that might flow from it, for we humans are sending a hundred or more rainforest species into extinction every day.

2 FALLEN TREE IN CLOUD FOREST, VENEZUELA (Stephen Dalton/OSF)
LIFE IN THE FOREST SILENTLY SEETHES WITH COMPETITION, SUCCESS AND FAILURE. SOMETIMES, SOUNDS LIKE GREAT PISTOL SHOTS ECHO THROUGH THE FOREST, FOLLOWED BY THE SPLINTERING, WHISTLING ROAR OF A FALLING TREE. A GAP HAS BEEN RIPPED IN THE GREEN SHROUD OF THE FOREST, AND LIGHT FLOODS IN TO ACTIVATE THE MANY SEEDLINGS OF THE FOREST FLOOR THAT HAVE BEEN WAITING FOR JUST SUCH AN OPPORTUNITY FOR YEARS SINCE THEIR HOPEFUL GERMINATION. A FURIOUS RACE BEGINS, AND LIFE FOAMS UPWARDS TO CLOSE OUT THE SKY ONCE MORE. 'NATURAL FELLING' OF THIS KIND ACTUALLY ENRICHES THE FOREST, ENCOURAGING COLONIZATION BY DIFFERENT SPECIES; CONVERSELY, COMMERCIAL LOGGING CAN DAMAGE THE FOREST IRREVOCABLY.

3   CLOUDED RAINFOREST, CAPARAO NATIONAL PARK, SOUTH EASTERN BRAZIL,
(Luiz Claudio Marigo)

4 AND 5   MIST-SHROUDED RAINFOREST, BRAZIL, (C. S. Caldicott/Remote Source)
AND INDONESIA (Tony Stone Photo Library)
HEAT FROM THE TROPICAL SUN, WARMING THE ATMOSPHERE TO BETWEEN
17°-30°C/64°-86°F COMBINES WITH HEAVY RAINFALL TO PROVIDE A HOTHOUSE
AMBIENCE. PLANTS, WHICH FORM THE FRAMEWORK OF TROPICAL RAINFOREST,
THRIVE IN THE WARM, MOIST ATMOSPHERE; ANIMALS CAN RELAX THEIR GUARD
AGAINST COLD AND DROUGHT. CONDITIONS FOR GROWTH ARE IDEAL, BUT IT IS
PART OF THE NATURAL ECOSYSTEM THAT THERE ARE HIDDEN COSTS AND
HAZARDS FOR ALL THE RAINFOREST'S ABUNDANT LIFE.

6 **LOWLAND RAINFOREST, COSTA RICA** (Michael and Patricia Fogden) WATER AND SUNLIGHT PROVIDE NOT ONLY THE HOTHOUSE ATMOSPHERE WHICH SO FAVOURS PLANT GROWTH, BUT ALSO THE VERY BASES OF LIFE ITSELF. ALL LIVING THINGS, PLANT OR ANIMAL, ARE MADE UP OF COUNTLESS CELLS WHICH ARE FORMED LARGELY OF WATER. WATER, TOO, TRANSPORTS THE NUTRIENTS OF THE FOREST BETWEEN PLANTS AND WITHIN THEM; AND WATER PLUS SUNLIGHT POWERS THE RAINFOREST. SOLAR ENERGY ALLOWS THE PLANT TO MAKE SUGARS FROM CARBON DIOXIDE DRAWN FROM THE AIR, AND FROM WATER – A PROCESS KNOWN AS PHOTOSYNTHESIS. THESE SUGARS ARE THE BUILDING BLOCKS OF MOLECULES WHICH MAKE UP THE PLANT'S CELLS, AND PROVIDE THE ENERGY THEY NEED FOR GROWTH.

7

8

7 **TRAFALGAR FALLS, DOMINICA, WEST INDIES** (Gerry Ellis/Ellis Wildlife Collection)

8 **IGUASSA FALLS, BRAZIL/ARGENTINA** (Michael and Patricia Fogden)

WATER IS THE LIFE-BLOOD OF THE RAINFOREST, BUT THERE IS A HIDDEN COST
TO ITS ABUNDANCE HERE. THE WATER PRIES EVERYWHERE, DISSOLVING AND
ERODING, BREAKING THINGS UP AND SUCKING THEIR MOLECULAR REMAINS –
ESSENTIAL FOR THE FOREST'S NUTRITION – OUT OF THE FOREST, INTO RIVERS,
AND OUT TO SEA. THE WATER THREATENS THE SUBSTANCE OF THE FOREST
ITSELF, ITS TISSUES, MINERALS AND BIOCHEMICALS, ITS FOOD AND ITS VERY
STRUCTURE. BUT THE FOREST HAS ADAPTED TO THIS PRESSURE OVER THE
MILLENNIA: NUTRIENTS ARE STOLEN FROM BODIES LIVING AND DEAD, AND
CLAWED BACK FROM THE WATER BEFORE THEY ARE LOST FOR EVER. ALL OF THE
FOREST'S MANY LIVES ARE GEARED TO THIS PERPETUAL OBLIGATION.

9

9   MOSSMAN RIVER GORGE, QUEENSLAND, AUSTRALIA (Leo Meier/Weldon Trannies)

10   TREE FERNS, TORO NEGRO, PUERTO RICO

(Gerry Ellis/Ellis Wildlife Collection)

THERE IS A GREATER WEIGHT OF VEGETATION IN EACH HECTARE OF TROPICAL
RAINFOREST THAN THERE IS IN THE SAME AREA OF ANY OTHER HABITAT ON
EARTH. UNDER THE BRIGHT TROPICAL SUN, THE RAINFOREST PRODUCES NEW
VEGETABLE TISSUES FASTER THAN ANY OTHER COMMUNITY ON LAND. THIS HIGH
PRODUCTIVITY IS BALANCED AND SUSTAINED BY DEATH – AS MUCH TISSUE DIES
AS IS PRODUCED, ITS DECAY YIELDING NUTRIENTS FOR RE-USE. THE RAINFOREST
IS THUS IN DYNAMIC BALANCE, ITS RATE OF TURNOVER FRANTIC BY THE
STANDARDS OF OTHER FORESTS IN DRIER OR COOLER REGIONS. HOWEVER, THE
FINELY TUNED BALANCE OF THE RAINFOREST SYSTEM IS VERY VULNERABLE
ONCE DISTURBED.

11

11 EMERGENT TREE, AMAZONIA
(Tony Morrison/South American Pictures)

**12 EMERGENT TREE OVER
CANOPY, KORUP NATIONAL PARK,
CAMEROON** (Phil Agland)
TROPICAL RAINFOREST NATURALLY
GROWS IN LOOSE 'TIERS' OF
VEGETATION, WHICH RANGE IN
HEIGHT FROM THE MINUTE TO THE
MONUMENTAL. 55M/180FT OR MORE
ABOVE THE GROUND, THE GIANT
TREES OF THE RAINFOREST, THE
EMERGENTS, THRUST INTO THE
SUNLIGHT. BELOW THEM IS THE
SPREADING SEA OF LEAVES KNOWN
AS THE CANOPY, FORMED BY A
DENSE LAYER OF TREES 15-30M/50-
100FT DEEP. THE CANOPY FORMS
THE BODY OF THE FOREST, AND IN
TURN SHADES THE SHRUBS AND
SMALL SAPLINGS BENEATH. THE
SEEDLINGS, FERNS AND FUNGI
COLONIZE THE FOREST FLOOR.

**13 SUNLIGHT, QUEENSLAND,
AUSTRALIA** (Leo Meier/Weldon Trannies)
VERY LITTLE SUNLIGHT ACTUALLY
REACHES THE FOREST FLOOR,
EXCEPT THROUGH GAPS CREATED
BY FALLEN TREES, OR THROUGH
THE SPACES CREATED BY
EMERGENTS PUSHING THROUGH
THE CANOPY, AND THE ODD CHINK
OPENED BY THE GENTLE
MOVEMENT OF THE WIND IN THE
MILLIONS OF LEAVES ABOVE.
EVERY TREE, EVERY SAPLING,
SHRUB AND SEEDLING, PUSHES
UPWARDS TO THE SUN, SEEKING TO
CAPTURE EVEN THE TINIEST RAY
FROM THE SOURCE OF ITS LIFE
AND ENERGY.

13

14 RAINFOREST TREE, QUEENSLAND, AUSTRALIA (Leo Meier/Weldon Trannies)
EVOLVED OVER MILLENNIA, AND OFTEN HUNDREDS OF YEARS OLD, RAINFOREST
TREES ARE FAR FROM BEING THE PASSIVE ORGANISMS THEY APPEAR. TREES SUCK
NUTRIENTS AND WATER FROM THE SOIL, AND ABSORB CARBON DIOXIDE FROM
THE ATMOSPHERE AND SUNLIGHT THROUGH THEIR LEAVES. TREES MUST FLOWER
AND ATTRACT POLLINATORS IN ORDER TO REPRODUCE; THEY MUST PRODUCE
FRUIT WHICH IS TEMPTING TO THE CREATURES WHO WILL DISPERSE THEIR SEEDS
TO ALL THE CORNERS OF THE FOREST AND ENSURE THE SURVIVAL OF THE
SPECIES. TREES MUST DEFEND THEMSELVES AGAINST PREDATORS, PARASITES
AND DISEASE PRODUCING ORGANISMS, AND TREES ARE THE FRAMEWORK OF THE
FOREST, THE STRUCTURE ON WHICH ALL OTHER LIFE RESTS: WITHOUT THE TREES
THE REST OF THE COMMUNITY CANNOT SURVIVE.

15 BUTTRESS ROOTS OF FOREST FIG TREE, SABAH, MALAYSIA
(Gerald Cubitt/Bruce Coleman Ltd)
THE ROOTS OF TREES SUCK UP ESSENTIAL NUTRIENTS AND MOISTURE FROM THE
SOIL, BUT THEY ALSO ANCHOR THE TREE SECURELY IN THE GROUND. HOWEVER,
THE ROOTS OF RAINFOREST TREES ARE OFTEN VERY NEAR THE SOIL SURFACE,
PERHAPS BECAUSE THIS IS WHERE THE GREATEST CONCENTRATION OF RICH
NUTRIENTS LIES. THESE SURFACE ROOTS MAY SUPPORT MONUMENTAL
STRUCTURES, OFTEN OVER 55M/180FT TALL, WHOSE WOOD IS HARD AND HEAVY –
THE PRIZE OF THE TROPICAL TIMBER TRADE. THE TREES' ENORMOUS BULK IS
STABILIZED BY BUTTRESS ROOTS, WHICH SPREAD THE WEIGHT OVER A WIDER AREA.

16

16   **RAINFOREST CANOPY FROM BELOW, MALAYSIA** (Earl of Cranbrook)
THE TREES OF THE CANOPY DO NOT TOUCH ONE ANOTHER, BUT NEATLY
INTERLOCK. THE REASON FOR THIS IS UNKNOWN – IT MAY BE TO PREVENT THE
SPREAD OF DISEASE, OR TO MAKE ACCESS FROM ONE TREE TO ANOTHER
DIFFICULT FOR PREDATORS. BUT TO ALL INTENTS AND PURPOSES THE CANOPY
FORMS A CLOSED LAYER, SHUTTING OUT THE SUN AND SHUTTING IN THE
MOISTURE. BELOW THE INSULATION OF THE CANOPY, THERE IS LITTLE SUNLIGHT
AND LITTLE WIND: TEMPERATURE AND HUMIDITY REMAIN MORE OR LESS EVEN,
DAY OR NIGHT, AND THE FOREST AIR IS BOTH COOLER AND MOISTER THAN
ABOVE THE TREES. WITHOUT THE CANOPY COVER AND THE WATER-RETAINING
PROPERTIES OF THE ROOTS OF THE FOREST PLANTS, THIS LUSH AND APPARENTLY
FERTILE GROUND IS QUICKLY AND IRREVOCABLY TURNED TO DESERT.

17   **CLIMBING FIG, BRAZIL** (Ken Preston-Mafham/Premaphotos)

18   *VICTORIA REGIA* **LILIES, AMAZONIA, BRAZIL** (C. S. Caldicott/Remote Source)
RAINFOREST PLANTS GROW IN A HUGE VARIETY OF WAYS: CLINGING, CLIMBING,
FLOATING, AND TWISTING THROUGH THE TREES. THE DIVERSITY OF PLANTS IN
THE RAINFOREST IS A SIGN OF ITS GREAT AGE. OVER MILLIONS OF YEARS THE
LIFE OF THE FOREST HAS EVOLVED INTO MANY FORMS WITH ENDLESS
REFINEMENTS FOR EXISTENCE IN A SPECIALISED ENVIRONMENT. THE RESULT IS
AN EXTRAORDINARY ARRAY OF DIVERSE SPECIES, MANY OF WHICH ARE NOW
BECOMING EXTINCT BEFORE THEY ARE EVEN DISCOVERED.

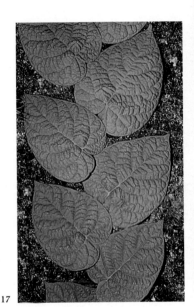

17

18

19

19 EYELASH VIPER ON PALM, COSTA RICA
(Michael and Patricia Fogden)
THIS EYELASH VIPER IS STRICTLY
TREE-DWELLING; LIKE ALL
RAINFOREST CREATURES, IT HAS
ITS OWN CLEARLY DEFINED NICHE
WITHIN THE ECOSYSTEM. THE
SNAKE IS ALSO COMPLETELY
DEPENDENT ON ITS ENVIRONMENT
IT IS ADAPTED TO FEED ON
RAINFOREST PREY, SURVIVE IN
RAINFOREST CLIMATE, AND HAS
EVOLVED TECHNIQUES OF
HUNTING AND HIDING ONLY
WITHIN THE RAINFOREST CONTEXT
IF IT LOSES THIS FRAMEWORK, THE
SNAKE, LIKE COUNTLESS OTHER
ANIMALS AND PLANTS, WOULD BE
UNABLE TO ADAPT TO THE SUDDEN
CHANGE AND WOULD FACE
CERTAIN EXTINCTION AS A SPECIES.

21

20   AERIAL ROOTS OF A FIG TREE, CAIRNS, AUSTRALIA (Weldon Trannies)

21   VARZÉA FLOODED FOREST, BRAZIL (Luiz Claudio Marigo)
WITHIN THE DIVERSE AND DYNAMIC ENVIRONMENT WHICH IS THE RAINFOREST,
MOST OF THE ACTION IS HIDDEN FROM VIEW. IT IS IMPOSSIBLE TO SAY HOW
MANY SPECIES OF PLANTS AND ANIMALS ARE CONTAINED IN THE VARZÉA
FLOODED FOREST, OR HOW MANY ARE SUPPORTED BY THE ABUNDANT FRUITS OF
THE FIG TREE. SCIENTIFIC STUDY OF THE LIFE OF THE RAINFOREST HAS ONLY
JUST BEGUN. SUCH RESEARCH OFFERS POTENTIALLY ENORMOUS REWARDS: BUT
WILL THE RAINFORESTS OF THE WORLD SURVIVE LONG ENOUGH FOR US TO
COMPLETE IT?

CHAPTER TWO

INFINITE VARIETY – A RICH DIVERSITY OF LIFE

DR TOM LOVEJOY

Tropical rainforests hold the greatest diversity of life of any environment on earth. Hidden by the vegetation from all but the trained eye are a multitude of plants and animals, rare, strange and beautiful. Among them are many species as yet undiscovered and unnamed, which may be of immense potential value to humanity; and there exist in the rainforest life forms which occur nowhere else in the world. What are the reasons for this extraordinary diversity of life, which we are in the process of eliminating before we even know its full extent?

T HE NUMBERS ARE ASTONISHING. THE AMAZON, WHICH drains the world's largest tropical rainforest, is thought to have about 3000 species of fish, including fruit-eating fish and the electric eel. This is more than are contained in the entire North Atlantic. The tropical forest country of Panama has 1500 species of butterfly, compared with 763 in the United States and a mere 68 in Great Britain. There are more species of woody plant on a single volcano in the Philippines than in the entire United States. Five times as many kinds of tree grow on the island of Madagascar as in the whole of temperate North America. The list is endless.

Given this bewildering and exhilarating variety, it is to the shame of modern science – and it is also perhaps its greatest critical challenge – that, while it has constructed devices with the potential to destroy civilization and most of biological diversity, it has failed so far to discover even to within an order of

---

22 CARNIVOROUS PITCHER PLANTS, MALAYSIA

(Gerald Cubitt/Bruce Coleman Ltd)

IT USED TO BE SAID THAT TROPICAL RAINFORESTS CONTAINED SOME HALF OF THE TOTAL NUMBER OF THE WORLD'S SPECIES. BUT IN THE LAST TWENTY YEARS, THE ESTIMATE OF THAT TOTAL NUMBER OF SPECIES HAS RISEN FROM THREE MILLION TO SIXTY MILLION. THE STUDIES WHICH HAVE LED TO THIS HUGELY INCREASED STATISTIC HAVE ALMOST ALL BEEN OF RAINFOREST LIFE. SOME SCIENTISTS NOW BELIEVE THAT THE TROPICAL RAINFORESTS OF THE WORLD MAY HOLD UP TO NINETY PER CENT OF THE PLANT AND ANIMAL SPECIES ON EARTH.

of organisms such as birds, butterflies and frogs have shown special areas where there are clusters of species which occur only in a limited range. These are thought by many to represent places where isolated patches of forest managed to survive in a succession of cool dry periods during the northern continents' Ice Age. In these areas, known as refuges, new species evolved. While this theory, which may help explain the origin of so much diversity in these forests, remains a hypothesis, it is beyond dispute that these areas contain species which occur nowhere else and hence should be priorities for conservation.

When the world's forests are being destroyed at a rate of close to forty hectares (100 acres) per minute, it is obviously important to act according to conservation priorities which already exist. Yet unless our knowledge of the flora and fauna of the tropical forests is increased rapidly and systematically, a great deal of biological diversity will slip through our fingers – and with it an incalculable reservoir of potential knowledge. In the field of medical science alone, the rainforests have yielded drugs effective against Hodgkin's disease, leukaemia and malaria, among many others.

The list of useful products of all sorts that derive from the forests is infinite, and new ones are being identified all the time. There is, moreover, the extraordinary potential of the dawning age of genetic engineering, a science that does not make new genes (contrary to myth), but depends on rearrangements of the existing ones. From this perspective, the ultimate wealth of the tropical nations is the genetic stock of their forests, from which incalculable and inconceivable benefits may be derived.

It is impossible to over-estimate the importance of the knowledge that stands to be lost with the biological diversity of these forests. For each species represents a unique combination of traits, each one of which is an evolutionary solution to biological problems. With each species lost, the potential growth of the life sciences is forever curtailed and impoverished. If we permit the loss of the rainforests, and with them a major portion of biological diversity, it might with justice be viewed as one of the greatest acts of desecration in human history.

---

23 ANGWANTIBO, WEST CENTRAL AFRICA (Phil Agland/Partridge Films)
THE RAINFOREST CAN BE SEEN AS A MOSAIC OF DIFFERENT MICRO-
ENVIRONMENTS WHICH MAKE UP THE GREATER WHOLE. THESE MICRO-
ENVIRONMENTS ARE CREATED BY DIFFERENT GROUPINGS OF VEGETATION, BY
THE HEIGHT OF THE HABITAT FROM THE GROUND (FOR INSTANCE, WHETHER
CANOPY OR SHRUB LAYER), BY AVAILABLE LIGHT, SOIL TYPE AND WETNESS. MOST
ANIMALS STAY FIRMLY WITHIN ONE OF THESE ENVIRONMENTS AND DO NOT
VENTURE INTO OTHERS: THUS MANY MONKEYS ALMOST NEVER DESCEND TO THE
GROUND, WHEREAS CERTAIN BIRDS NEVER GO HIGHER THAN THE SHRUB LAYER.
THIS HELPS TO REDUCE COMPETITION WITH OTHER SPECIES WHICH MAY HAVE
SIMILAR REQUIREMENTS; SO WHILE THE INSECT-EATING ANGWANTIBO OCCUPIES
THE LOW SHRUB LAYER OF THE FOREST, THE POTTO, ANOTHER PRIMATE WHICH
EATS INSECTS AND FRUITS, LIVES IN THE FOREST CANOPY. THE TWO WILL NEVER
NEED TO VIE FOR FOOD.

24 MONTANE FOREST, EASTERN
ANDES (Tony Morrison/South American
Pictures)
RAINFOREST IS A GENERIC TERM
ENCOMPASSING A WIDE RANGE OF
FOREST TYPES. THEY ARE
CLASSIFIED ACCORDING TO
FACTORS SUCH AS SOIL TYPE,
SEASONALITY, AND ALTITUDE INTO
AS MANY AS FORTY FOREST
FORMATIONS. BECAUSE
KNOWLEDGE OF THE SPECIES
WITHIN RAINFORESTS IS STILL SO
LIMITED, THIS CLASSIFICATION IS
USEFUL FOR CONSERVATION
PURPOSES. IF A CROSS-SECTION OF
FOREST TYPES WERE PRESERVED,
THIS WOULD ENSURE THAT THEIR
VARIOUS INHABITANTS WOULD
ALSO SURVIVE. THE TERM
'MONTANE' INCLUDES SEVERAL
FURTHER FOREST TYPES, SUCH AS
ELFIN, WHERE THE TREES ARE
STUNTED AND TWISTED BY HIGH
WINDS, AND CLOUD FOREST,
WHERE THE ALTITUDE IS SUCH
THAT CLOUD ENCIRCLES THE
TREES IN SWIRLING MIST AND THE
HUMIDITY IS VERY HIGH.

25

25 BUTTRESS ROOTS AND LIANAS, LOWLAND RAINFOREST, PERU
(Michael and Patricia Fogden)
THE WORD 'RAINFOREST' IS GENERALLY UNDERSTOOD TO MEAN THE LOWLAND
OR LOW MONTANE TYPE, SUCH AS IS FOUND IN THE AMAZON BASIN, IN WEST
CENTRAL AFRICA, AND IN PARTS OF SOUTH EAST ASIA. IT IS THIS FOREST WHICH
HAS THE GREATEST SPECIES DIVERSITY, IS LEAST SEASONAL AND HAS MAINLY
EVERGREEN GROWTH. HOWEVER, THIS SHOULD NOT BE TAKEN TO MEAN THAT
LOWLAND IS THE ONLY KIND OF RAINFOREST WORTHY OF NOTE OR STUDY – AND
IT CERTAINLY SHOULD NOT BE IMAGINED THAT IT IS THE ONLY RAINFOREST TYPE
WHICH IS UNDER THREAT.

26

26 FLOODED GALLERY FOREST, VENEZUELA

(Sullivan & Rogers/Bruce Coleman Ltd)

THE GALLERY FORESTS ARE CORRIDORS OF RAINFOREST-LIKE GROWTH
BORDERING RIVERS WHICH FLOW THROUGH OTHERWISE NON-RAINFOREST
REGIONS. THIS LUXURIANT GROWTH MAY BE ONLY A FEW KILOMETRES WIDE
FROM THE RIVER TO ITS GRASSLAND EDGE, BUT STILL HARBOURS MANY OF THE
SPECIES FOUND IN THE NEARBY AMAZON BASIN. GALLERY FOREST, LIKE SOME
AUSTRALIAN RAINFOREST, SOME BRAZILIAN ATLANTIC COAST REGIONS AND SOME
FORESTS ELSEWHERE IN SOUTH AMERICA, TENDS TO BE STRONGLY SEASONAL.
UNLIKE SOME RAINFORESTS WHICH HAVE HEAVY RAINFALL ALMOST ALL THE
YEAR, THESE FORESTS HAVE A DISTINCT DRY SEASON, DURING WHICH THE
DECIDUOUS TREES, OF WHICH THERE ARE MANY, DROP THEIR LEAVES.

27 GIANT TREE FERNS, ATLANTIC FOREST, SOUTHERN BRAZIL

(Luiz Claudio Marigo)

THE ATLANTIC RAINFOREST OF COASTAL BRAZIL IS QUITE DISTINCT FROM THAT OF THE BRAZILIAN AMAZON. SEPARATED BY NON-RAINFOREST TERRAIN, THE TWO FORESTS HAVE EVOLVED INDEPENDENTLY WITH ONLY A LIMITED OVERLAP OF SPECIES. TREE FERNS FAVOUR VERY WET FOREST AND NEED PLENTY OF LIGHT, PIONEERING GROWTH IN THE GAPS CREATED BY FALLEN TREES. THEY CAN REACH 20M/65FT IN HEIGHT. THERE ARE AT LEAST 700 SPECIES OF TREE FERN THROUGHOUT THE TROPICS AND SUBTROPICS, SOME GROWING IN ONLY A VERY LIMITED RANGE. HUGE CHUNKS OF BRAZIL'S ATLANTIC RAINFOREST HAVE BEEN CLEARED FOR CATTLE RANCHING AND IT IS NOW IN IMMINENT DANGER OF EXTINCTION.

28

28 SLOW LORIS, MALAYSIA (Gerald Cubitt/Bruce Coleman Ltd)
IT IS RARE FOR TWO KINDS OF ANIMAL IN ONE FOREST TO HAVE EXACTLY THE
SAME NEEDS IN ONE FOREST – TO OCCUPY THE SAME ECOLOGICAL 'NICHE'. A
'NICHE' IS THE ANIMAL'S SLOT IN THE ECOSYSTEM: WHAT IT EATS, WHERE IT
LIVES IN THE FOREST, WHAT PREYS ON IT, AND SO ON. EQUIVALENT NICHES SEEM
TO EXIST IN GEOGRAPHICALLY SEPARATE RAINFORESTS, BUT CAN BE OCCUPIED
BY ONE SPECIES IN AFRICA AND QUITE ANOTHER IN THE AMERICAS. HOWEVER,
THE ANIMALS EVOLVE PHYSICALLY TO EXPLOIT THESE NICHES AND TEND TO
LOOK ALIKE: COMPARE THIS LORIS WITH THE UNRELATED AFRICAN ANGWANTIBO
ON PAGE 39.

29

29 TAMANDUA ANTEATER, AMAZON BASIN, PERU
(Michael and Patricia Fogden)

30 GIANT PANGOLIN, SOUTH EASTERN CAMEROON
(Lisa Silcock/Dja River Films)
THE SOUTH AMERICAN TAMANDUA AND THE AFRICAN PANGOLIN ILLUSTRATE THE WAY THAT DIFFERENT SPECIES WITH SIMILAR REQUIREMENTS TEND TO EVOLVE THE SAME PHYSICAL CHARACTERISTICS WHICH BEST SUIT THEIR LIFE-STYLE. THIS THEORY IS KNOWN AS CONVERGENT EVOLUTION. THUS BOTH ANIMALS, WHICH SPECIALIZE IN EATING ANTS AND TERMITES (THE GIANT PANGOLIN CAN CONSUME 200,000 ANTS A NIGHT, WEIGHING SOME 700G/1½LB), HAVE EVOLVED NARROW HEADS, TOOTHLESS MOUTHS AND LONG,

NARROW, STICKY TONGUES WITH WHICH TO PROBE THE NESTS OF ANTS AND TERMITES, AND MASSIVE CLAWS FOR DIGGING COMPACTED MOUNDS. BOTH PANGOLIN AND ANTEATER ARE ENDANGERED: PANGOLIN MEAT IS PRIZED, WHILE TAMUNDUAS ARE KILLED ON ROADS IN DEVELOPED AREAS OR FOR SPORT; AND CERTAIN ANTEATER SPECIES ARE COLLECTED FOR THE LIVE ANIMAL TRADE. BUT DESTRUCTION OF THEIR HABITAT MAY PROVE AN EVEN GREATER THREAT.

30

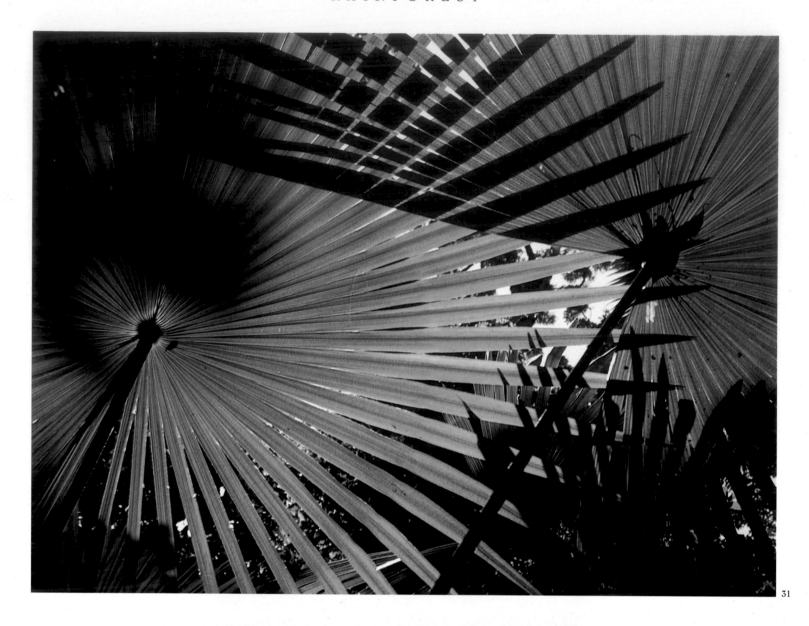

31

32

33

31 **FAN PALM LEAVES** (Simon Bracken/Weldon Trannies)

32 **RAINFOREST HERB LAYER, COSTA RICA** (Michael Fogden/Bruce Coleman Ltd)

33 **HELICONIA LEAVES, MONTEVERDE, COSTA RICA** (Michael Fogden/Bruce Coleman Ltd)
THE DIVERSITY OF RAINFOREST PLANT LIFE IS STAGGERING: IN A TYPICAL PATCH
OF RAINFOREST JUST 6.5KM/4 MILES SQUARE, THERE CAN BE AS MANY AS 1500
SPECIES OF FLOWERING PLANT AND 750 SPECIES OF TREE. IN THE MONTEVERDE
FOREST AREA OF COSTA RICA, WHERE TWO OF THESE PICTURES WERE TAKEN,
THERE ARE AN ESTIMATED 2500 SPECIES OF PLANT. COMPARE THE FIGURES FOR A
10-HECTARE/25-ACRE PLOT OF TEMPERATE FOREST, WHICH MIGHT YIELD FIFTEEN
OR, AT MOST, THIRTY TREE SPECIES: AN EQUIVALENT AREA OF AMAZON
RAINFOREST CONTAINS SOME 300. MANY OF THESE PLANTS HAVE NOT EVEN BEEN
NAMED, AND ALMOST NONE HAVE BEEN INVESTIGATED SCIENTIFICALLY. GIVEN
THAT OVER FORTY PER CENT OF DRUGS PRESCRIBED IN THE US OWE THEIR
POTENCY TO 'NATURAL' CHEMICALS, MAINLY FROM RAINFOREST PLANTS, HOW
MANY POSSIBLY REVOLUTIONARY DRUGS COULD WE BE LOSING DAY BY DAY
WITH EACH HECTARE OF RAINFOREST?

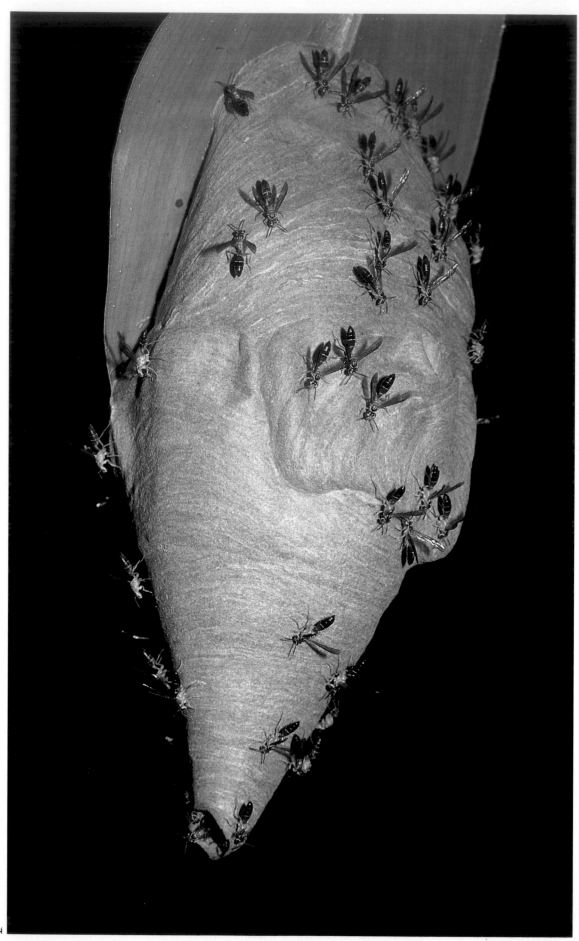

34 SOCIAL WASPS, TRINIDAD
(Ken Preston-Mafham/Premaphotos)
THESE COMMON RAINFOREST
WASPS ARE ONE OF A HUGE RANGE
OF TROPICAL FOREST SPECIES.
THEIR NESTS, WHICH ARE
CONSTRUCTED LIKE THOSE OF
EUROPEAN WASPS FROM WOOD
SCRAPINGS, ARE SUSPENDED
UNDER BROAD LEAVES TO PROVIDE
SHELTER. FROM THIS PROTECTED
POSITION THE WASPS ARE QUICK
TO SWARM OUT OF THE ENTRANCE
TO THE NEST AT THE SLIGHTEST
DISTURBANCE AND INTO
DEFENSIVE POSTURE, ABDOMENS
ERECT, READY TO STING. THIS
STRATEGY AND THEIR PAINFUL
STINGS MAKE THEM A RARE PREY:
THEIR ONLY SERIOUS ENEMIES ARE
THE COLONIES OF ARMY ANTS
RAMPAGING THROUGH THE
FOREST. AN ARMY ANT RAID WILL
CLEAN THE NEST OF EGGS, LARVAE,
FOOD STORES AND ANY WASP
UNABLE TO ESCAPE. THE REST OF
THE COLONY SWARM NEARBY,
HELPLESS IN THE FACE OF THE
PLUNDERERS.

**35 ARMY ANTS CARRYING WASP
LARVA, COSTA RICA**
(Michael and Patricia Fogden)
ARMY ANTS ARE FAMOUS FOR
THEIR SPECTACULAR PREDATORY
RAIDS. THE COLONIES OF SOME
SPECIES CAN NUMBER UP TO TWO
MILLION, WHILE IN AFRICA THE
SIMILAR DRIVER ANT COLONIES
MAY NUMBER TWENTY MILLION.
THESE CARNIVOROUS ANTS FORAGE
MAINLY ON THE FOREST FLOOR,
WHERE THEY PIN DOWN AND
CARRY OFF ANY INSECT TOO TARDY
TO MOVE AWAY FROM THE
ENDLESS COLUMN WHICH CAN
NUMBER UP TO 50,000 INDIVIDUALS.
ANTS HAVE A HIGHLY DEVELOPED
SOCIAL ORDER IN WHICH EACH
CASTE, WHETHER QUEEN, WORKER
OR SOLDIER, HAS ITS OWN SPECIFIC
ROLE, AND IN EVOLUTIONARY
TERMS THEY ARE HIGHLY
SUCCESSFUL INSECTS. THERE ARE
LITERALLY THOUSANDS OF SPECIES
OF ANTS IN THE WORLD'S TROPICAL
RAINFORESTS; THEY HAVE
COLONIZED EVERY PART OF IT
FROM FLOOR TO CANOPY.

34

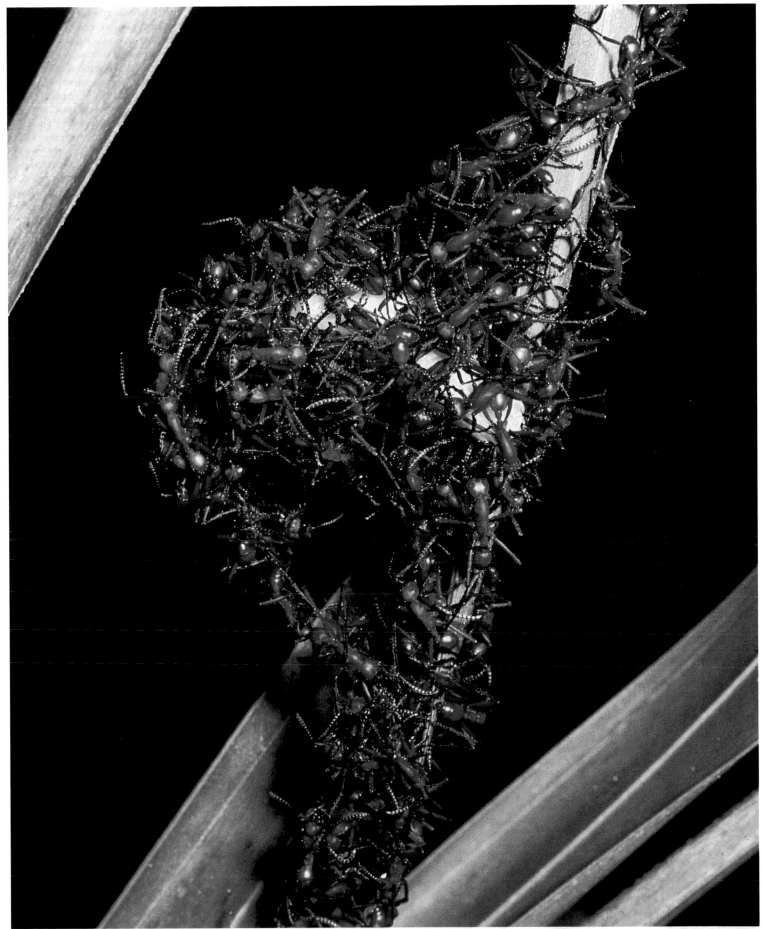

35

41

AT LEAST HALF THE WORLD'S 8,500 SPECIES OF BIRDS LIVE IN TROPICAL RAINFOREST. AFTER INSECTS, BIRDS ARE THE GREATEST EXPRESSION OF THE DIVERSITY OF THE FOREST, OCCUPYING EVERY AVAILABLE NICHE IN THE SYSTEM. IN TROPICAL FOREST, BIRDS OF SEVERAL DIFFERENT SPECIES WILL FORAGE THROUGH THE FOREST TOGETHER IN PARTIES FOR MUTUAL BENEFIT. THUS INSECT-EATING BIRDS WILL CLUSTER AROUND FRUIT-EATERS, WHOSE PECKING DISTURBS THE INSECTS. A GREATER NUMBER OF INDIVIDUALS ALSO GIVES BETTER PROTECTION AGAINST PREDATORS.

42

41 RED-NECKED TANAGER
(Luiz Claudio Marigo)

42 SEVEN-COLOURED TANAGER
(Luiz Claudio Marigo)
THERE ARE HUNDREDS OF SPECIES OF TANAGER THROUGHOUT THE NEW WORLD - 220 EXIST IN SOUTH AMERICA ALONE – AND BY FAR THE MAJORITY HAVE THEIR HOME IN TROPICAL RAINFORESTS. EXTRAVAGANTLY COLOURED, MAINLY FRUIT-EATING BIRDS, TANAGERS TEND TO HAVE NARROW ECOLOGICAL NICHES. DIFFERENT SPECIES LIVE AT DIFFERENT ALTITUDES: THEIR NUMBERS INDICATE THE DIVERSITY OF HABITATS WHICH EXIST WITHIN THE RAINFOREST. THEIR NEED FOR SPECIFIC ENVIRONMENTS MEANS THAT MANY SPECIES CAN LIVE IN CLOSE PROXIMITY WITHOUT HAVING TO COMPETE FOR FOOD.

43

43 GREEN HONEY CREEPER
(Luiz Claudio Marigo)
THE HONEY CREEPER IS PART OF
THE TANAGER FAMILY, THOUGH IT
SEEMS TO BE MORE ADAPTABLE
THAN THE TANAGERS THEMSELVES:
IT CAN LIVE IN BOTH PRISTINE
TROPICAL FOREST AND SECONDARY
GROWTH, AND IT FORAGES FOR
FOOD IN A RANGE OF HABITATS,
FROM THE LOWER LEVELS OF THE
FOREST TO THE TREE TOPS, EITHER
ALONE OR IN GROUPS.

**44 LOTEN'S SUNBIRD (MALE), SRI
LANKA**
(Dieter and Mary Plage/Bruce Coleman Ltd)
THE SUNBIRD OCCUPIES THE SAME
ECOLOGICAL NICHE IN THE OLD
WORLD AS THE HUMMINGBIRD IN
CENTRAL AND SOUTH AMERICA,
AND RANGES FROM AFRICA TO
ASIA. LIKE THE HUMMINGBIRDS,
THEY ARE TINY, OFTEN
IRIDESCENT, JEWEL-LIKE DRINKERS
OF NECTAR, BUT THE TWO GROUPS
ARE NOT AT ALL RELATED.

44

48 GOLDEN BEETLE, CLOUD FOREST, COSTA RICA
(Michael and Patricia Fogden)
IT IS NOT KNOWN HOW MANY BEETLE SPECIES EXIST IN THE RAINFOREST, BUT THE NUMBER IS WITHOUT DOUBT PHENOMENAL. BEETLES ACCOUNT FOR THE LARGEST PROPORTION OF ANIMAL DIVERSITY IN THE RAINFOREST: SO FAR ONLY A COMPARATIVELY FEW SPECIES HAVE BEEN ENUMERATED. EVEN A REMOTELY ACCURATE ESTIMATE MIGHT GIVE US A CLUE TO THE REAL LEVEL OF SPECIES DIVERSITY IN THIS UNCHARTED ENVIRONMENT.

48

49 FEMALE MARSUPIAL FROG, CLOUD FOREST, VENEZUELA
(Michael and Patricia Fogden)
THE FEMALE MARSUPIAL FROG LAYS HER EGGS, WHICH ARE THEN FERTILIZED BY THE MALE WHO INSERTS THEM INTO A SAC ON HER BACK. THIS SEALS OVER, CREATING A MOIST AND PROTECTED ENVIRONMENT IN WHICH THE EGGS CAN MATURE. AFTER SOME FOUR WEEKS THE SEETHING, WRIGGLING, FULLY FORMED FROGLETS EMERGE. THIRTY-TWO FROGLETS CAME OUT OF THE SAC OF THIS FEMALE.

49

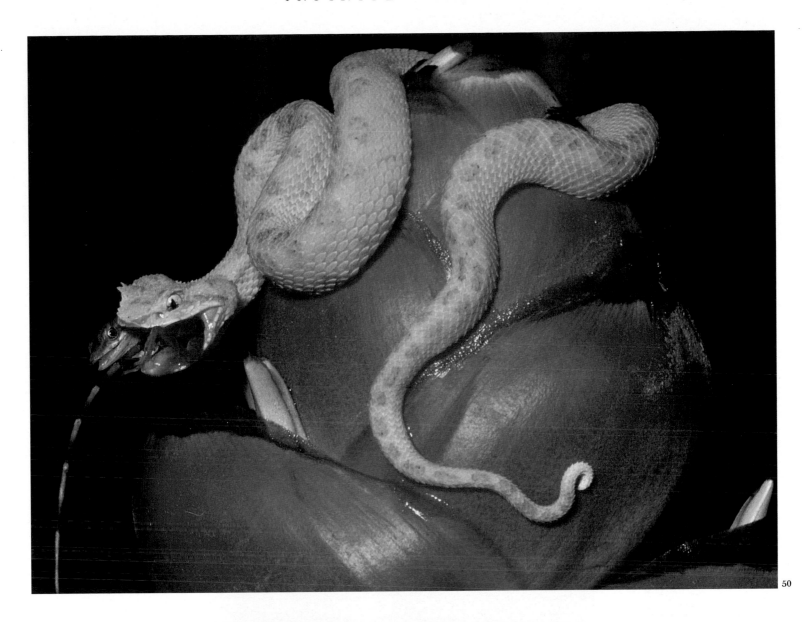

50

50 EYELASH VIPER KILLING
ANOLE ON HELICONIA FLOWER,
COSTA RICA
(Michael and Patricia Fogden)
THE EYELASH VIPER OCCURS IN A
VARIETY OF COLOURS, THE MOST
SPECTACULAR BEING THIS GOLDEN
YELLOW. IT USES ITS COLOUR AS A
LURE; SMALL BIRDS, FOR INSTANCE,
ARE ATTRACTED BY THE
BRIGHTNESS; BUT AN
INVESTIGATION OF IT MAY PROVE
FATAL. SPECIALIZED KILLERS,
VENOMOUS SNAKES LIKE THE
VIPERS ARE AMONG THE MANY
RAINFOREST PLANTS AND ANIMALS
WHICH USE POISON BOTH TO
DEFEND THEMSELVES AND TO
HUNT.

51

51 WEEVIL ON GINGER FLOWER,
COSTA RICA
(Ken Preston-Mafham/Premaphotos)
WEEVILS, CHARACTERIZED BY
THEIR LONG SNOUTS, ARE
COMMON IN RAINFORESTS
THROUGHOUT THE TROPICS.
WEEVILS BORE THEIR SNOUTS INTO
THE FLESHY PARTS OF SEEDS AND
PLANTS TO FEED; THE HOLE ALSO
MAKES A SAFE DEPOSIT FOR THE
FEMALE'S EGGS.

53

52 **LAR GIBBON AND YOUNG, SOUTH EAST ASIA** (Rod Williams/Bruce Coleman Ltd)

53 **BLACK HOWLER MONKEY, SOUTH AMERICA** (Rod Williams/Bruce Coleman Ltd)
MONKEYS ARE AT THEIR MOST DIVERSE IN TROPICAL RAINFORESTS, AND ARE
SUPREME EXPLOITERS OF THEIR ARBOREAL ENVIRONMENT. THE HOWLER
MONKEY ALMOST NEVER DESCENDS BELOW THE MIDDLE STOREY OF THE
FOREST, WHILE THE LAR GIBBON, LIKE THE OTHER GIBBONS, IS AMONG THE
FASTEST OF ALL FOREST ANIMALS THROUGH THE TREE-TOPS. PERFECTLY
ADAPTED, THEY CAN ACHIEVE GREAT SPEEDS AS THEY SWING ARM TO ARM
THROUGH THE CANOPY OF TREES, SOMETIMES LEAPING 15M/ALMOST 50 FEET AT A
TIME.

CHAPTER THREE

THE TROPICAL ARMS RACE – STRATEGIES FOR SURVIVAL
P. MICK RICHARDSON

The rainforest is not merely a random collection of plants and animals but a highly complex interactive community. Trees provide the framework for this community, supporting it in a huge variety of ways. Throughout the rainforest ecosystem, however, there is continual conflict between species, and no conflict has shaped the forest so profoundly as the evolutionary battle between the trees and the herbivores. Their war has been fought with chemicals, and has been played out through the millennia in tropical forests all over the world.

THE TREES AND OTHER RAINFOREST PLANTS, WHICH build themselves almost from thin air, forming organic compounds from sunlight, atmospheric carbon dioxide and water, constitute the first link in the food chain. They are thus the primary requirement of life for the next link in the chain: the huge numbers of plant-eating insects and other herbivores in the forest. Finding themselves in the front line of the battle for survival, these plants are faced with a dilemma. For at the same time as needing to attract beneficial pollinators and seed dispersers, they must also minimize the damage caused by the

54 CATERPILLARS OF LYCAENID BUTTERFLY FEEDING ON CYCAD LEAF, COSTA RICA (Michael and Patricia Fogden)
THE GREATEST POTENTIAL THREAT TO THE HEALTH OF THE FOREST IS POSED BY THE HERBIVORES: UNTRAMMELLED, THEY WOULD DECIMATE EVERY PLANT. HOWEVER, OVER THE MILLENNIA THE RAINFOREST PLANTS HAVE EVOLVED DEFENCES BOTH STRUCTURAL AND CHEMICAL: IN MANY TREES, EVERY LEAF, ROOT, FRUIT AND FLOWER, THE BARK AND THE WOOD ARE PROTECTED BY A POISONOUS OR DISTASTEFUL COMPOUND. BUT THEIR PREDATORS HAVE RESPONDED. SUCCESSIVE GENERATIONS HAVE ADAPTED TO DEAL WITH THE DEFENCES, PROVOKING ONGOING 'CHEMICAL WARFARE' BETWEEN PLANT AND PREDATOR. AS A RESULT ANIMALS HAVE EVOLVED WHICH SPECIALIZE IN FEEDING ON ONLY ONE OR TWO KINDS OF PLANT THAT WOULD BE DEADLY TO OTHERS. ONLY THE CATERPILLARS SHOWN HERE, ALONG WITH ONE BEETLE SPECIES, ARE ABLE TO EAT THE LEAVES OF THIS HIGHLY TOXIC CYCAD. THE CATERPILLARS ACTUALLY SYNTHESIZE THE INGESTED LEAF POISONS AND USE THEM FOR THEIR OWN DEFENCE: THEIR COLOURATION WARNS POTENTIAL PREDATORS THAT THEY ARE DANGEROUS.

70

56

57

56 YOUNG LEAVES OF CERCROPIA TREE, SOUTH AMERICA
(Tony Morrison/South American Pictures)

57 MAIDENHAIR FERN, TRINIDAD (Ken Preston-Mafham/Premaphotos)
YOUNG LEAVES ARE PARTICULARLY VULNERABLE TO PREDATORS, AS IT IS OFTEN
SOME TIME BEFORE THEY TOUGHEN AND DEVELOP THEIR DEFENSIVE
COMPOUNDS. RED PIGMENTATION IS COMMON IN YOUNG LEAVES; IN THE
CANOPY, THE PIGMENT MAY BE A PROTECTION AGAINST THE HARSH RAYS OF THE
SUN. ITS CHEMICAL BASE, ANTHOCYANIN, ALSO FORMS THE BUILDING-BLOCKS
FOR THE DEFENSIVE COMPOUNDS WHICH DEVELOP AS THE LEAF MATURES.

63

63 LIMACODIDAE MOTH LARVAE, VENEZUELA (Ken Preston-Mafham/Premaphotos)
CATERPILLARS, WHICH ARE SOFT AND SLOW MOVING, OFTEN STAYING ON THE
SAME LEAF FOR LONG PERIODS OF TIME, ARE POTENTIALLY EXTREMELY
VULNERABLE TO PREDATORS. BUT MANY OF THEM HAVE EVOLVED DEFENCES
WHICH DETER ALL BUT THE MOST INEXPERIENCED OF ANIMALS. THE
LIMACODIDAE MAY WARN OF THEIR VERY PAINFULLY STINGING HAIRS WITH
THEIR BRIGHT GREEN 'COATS', THOUGH GREEN IS NOT USUALLY A WARNING
COLOUR.

64

65

66

64 BUTTERFLY CATERPILLAR, CAMEROON
(Michael Fogden/Bruce Coleman Ltd))

65 LIMACODIDAE MOTH LARVA, JAVA (Ken Preston-Mafham/Premaphotos)

66 NYMPHALIDAE BUTTERFLY LARVA, MALAYSIA
(Ken Preston-Mafham/Premaphotos)
MANY CATERPILLARS HAVE STINGING SPINES, WHICH EVEN TO A HUMAN CAN CAUSE SPORADIC ITCHING FOR UP TO A YEAR. THESE SPINES, WHICH IN SOME CASES TRAIL ONTO THE LEAF, BLUR ITS OUTLINE AND HENCE THE SHADOW WHICH MIGHT OTHERWISE GIVE IT AWAY. ALTHOUGH THE CATERPILLARS' BASIC COLOURS ARE CRYPTIC (MOSTLY GREEN TO MERGE WITH THE LEAVES ON WHICH THEY FEED), ON CLOSER INSPECTION A PREDATOR WOULD BE ALERTED TO DISCREET WARNING COLORATION, SUCH AS THE YELLOW AND BLACK BELT, AND THE YELLOW TIPPED SPINES

68

69

67 BUTTERFLY CHRYSALIS, CENTRAL AMERICA (Partridge Films) THE CATERPILLAR SPENDS ITS ENTIRE LARVAL STAGE EATING AND GROWING, PREPARATORY TO PUPATING. SUSPENDED FROM A LEAF OR BRANCH, THE CHRYSALIS DEVELOPS IN WHICH THE METAMORPHOSIS FROM CATERPILLAR TO BUTTERFLY OR MOTH TAKES PLACE. WHEN THE ADULT FINALLY EMERGES, IT WILL NO LONGER EAT LEAVES BUT IT IS THOUGHT THAT SOME CATERPILLARS WHICH FEED ON TOXIC PLANTS AND STORE POISONS FOR THEIR OWN PROTECTION MAY MAINTAIN THESE DEFENCES THROUGH METAMORPHOSIS, THUS CONFERRING THEM ON THE NEW BUTTERFLY OR MOTH.

68 SWALLOWTAIL BUTTERFLY LARVA MIMICKING BIRD DROPPING, PANAMA (Ken Preston-Mafham/Premaphotos) LIKE MANY RAINFOREST CREATURES, SOME CATERPILLARS CHOOSE DISGUISE AS A DEFENCE AGAINST PREDATORS, RATHER THAN STINGING SPINES OR TOXIC COMPOUNDS. THIS LARVA, GIVING NO CLUE TO THE SPECTACULAR BUTTERFLY IT WILL BECOME, INNOCUOUSLY IMITATES A BIRD DROPPING.

69 MOTH LARVA, BOLIVIA (G.I. Bernard/NHPA) THE HAIRS ON THIS ENCLEIDAE MOTH CATERPILLAR CAN INFLICT A VICIOUS STING ON THE UNWARY – ANIMAL OR HUMAN.

70

70 UNIDENTIFIED FLOWER,
MONTANE FOREST, AMAZON/ANDES
(Tony Morrison/South American Pictures)

71 RAIN ON LEAVES, JAVA
(Alain Compost/Bruce Coleman Ltd)
AS WELL AS DEFENDING
THEMSELVES FROM PREDATORS,
RAINFOREST PLANTS MUST GUARD
AGAINST THE WATER WHICH IS
EVERYWHERE. WATER POOLING ON
THE LEAF COULD ENCOURAGE THE
FORMATION OF ALGAL GROWTH,
WHICH WOULD BLOCK LIFE-GIVING
SUNLIGHT FROM ITS HOST.
HOWEVER, WATER IS QUICKLY
CHANNELLED AWAY VIA THE 'DRIP
TIPS' OF THE LEAVES SHOWN HERE,
WHICH ARE CHARACTERISTIC OF
RAINFOREST PLANTS: ALSO
COMMON IS A WAXY, SHINY LEAF
SURFACE, WHICH AIDS WATER
RUNOFF AND MAKES THE LEAF
TOUGHER FOR PREDATORS TO EAT.

71

72

73

72   THORNS ON SAPLING, MARACÁ
(William Milliken/Royal Geographic Society
Maracá Rainforest Project)
THE DEFENCES EVOLVED BY
PLANTS AGAINST THEIR PREDATORS
MAY BE STRUCTURAL AS WELL AS
CHEMICAL, AND THOUGH
CLUMSIER MAY BE JUST AS
EFFECTIVE AS LEAF COMPOUNDS.
THE THORNS ON THE TRUNK OF
THIS SAPLING ARE AN EFFECTIVE
DETERRENT. IN SOME TREE
SPECIES, THORNS ARE PRESENT ON
THE SAPLING BUT ARE SHED WHEN
THE MATURE TREE DEVELOPS
DEFENSIVE CHEMICAL COMPOUNDS.

73 RESIN OF PTEROCARPUS SOYAUXII, CAMEROON (Mike Harrison/Dja River Films)
ALL TREES HAVE RESINOUS SAP WHICH QUICKLY RISES TO SEAL ANY WOUNDS OR
ABRASIONS IN THE BARK OR WOOD. THIS IS IMPORTANT IN PREVENTING EITHER
AN INFECTION ENTERING THE PLANT, OR INSECTS TRYING TO COLONIZE THE
UNPROTECTED WOOD BENEATH THE BARK. THE STINGLESS BEES SHOWN HERE
ARE GATHERING THE OOZING RESIN FOR USE IN THE DEFENCE OF THEIR OWN
NEST ENTRANCE.

CHAPTER FOUR

THE UNWITTING MATCHMAKERS: FERTILIZATION BY MANIPULATION
PROFESSOR GHILLEAN T. PRANCE

Once the plant has successfully defended itself against predators, its second imperative must be to reproduce. For the flowering trees, shrubs and herbs, fertilization must first take place: pollen grains from male flower parts need to be transferred to the female flower parts. But plants cannot move and so must find other means of transporting their pollen. Many employ animals, birds, bats and insects in particular, as carriers. But how can a simple plant manipulate such creatures into helping it to reproduce? The secret lies in its flowers: each one is an alluring target whose colour, scent and structure is designed to attract a specific, though unwitting, pollinator.

MOST FLOWERING PLANT SPECIES MUST BE POLLI-nated in order to produce seed. The dust-like pollen grains of the flower are its sperm which must be carried to the ovule of another flower in order to fertilize it. In temperate oak and pine forests this process is relatively straightforward; but in tropical rainforests where individual trees of any species are scattered throughout the forest in order to protect themselves from predators and fungal diseases, the process is more complicated. Wind pollination, so successful in temperate regions, here will not work, not only because of the distances involved but also because of the dense canopy under which the air hangs motionless. Rainforest plants therefore rely on animals and in-

---

74 EUGLOSSINE BEE LEAVING ORCHID WITH POLLEN, COSTA RICA
(David Thompson/OSF)

THE INTERDEPENDENCE OF RAINFOREST SPECIES IS EPITOMIZED BY THE RELATIONSHIP BETWEEN SEVERAL TYPES OF ORCHID AND THEIR POLLINATORS. CLEARLY, MANY ANIMALS DEPEND ON PLANTS FOR FOOD; EQUALLY, MANY PLANTS DEPEND ON ANIMALS, IN SOME CASES A SINGLE SPECIES, IN ORDER TO REPRODUCE. THIS ORCHID NEEDS THE ATTENTION OF THE MALE OF THIS BEE SPECIES TO FERTILIZE IT BY CARRYING ITS POLLEN TO ANOTHER FLOWER: ITS ENTIRE STRUCTURE IS GEARED TOWARDS TRAPPING THE BEE, REMOVING POLLEN IT IS ALREADY CARRYING AND STICKING ITS OWN POLLEN ONTO THE BEE'S BODY. IN RETURN, IT PROVIDES THE BEE WITH AN ARRAY OF EXOTIC PERFUMES WHICH THE BEE WILL USE IN TURN TO ATTRACT FEMALES. LIKE MANY OTHER RAINFOREST PLANTS AND ANIMALS, NEITHER ORCHID NOR BEE COULD SURVIVE WITHOUT THE OTHER, A GRAPHIC EXAMPLE OF THE COMPLEXITY AND FRAGILITY OF THE RAINFOREST ECOSYSTEM.

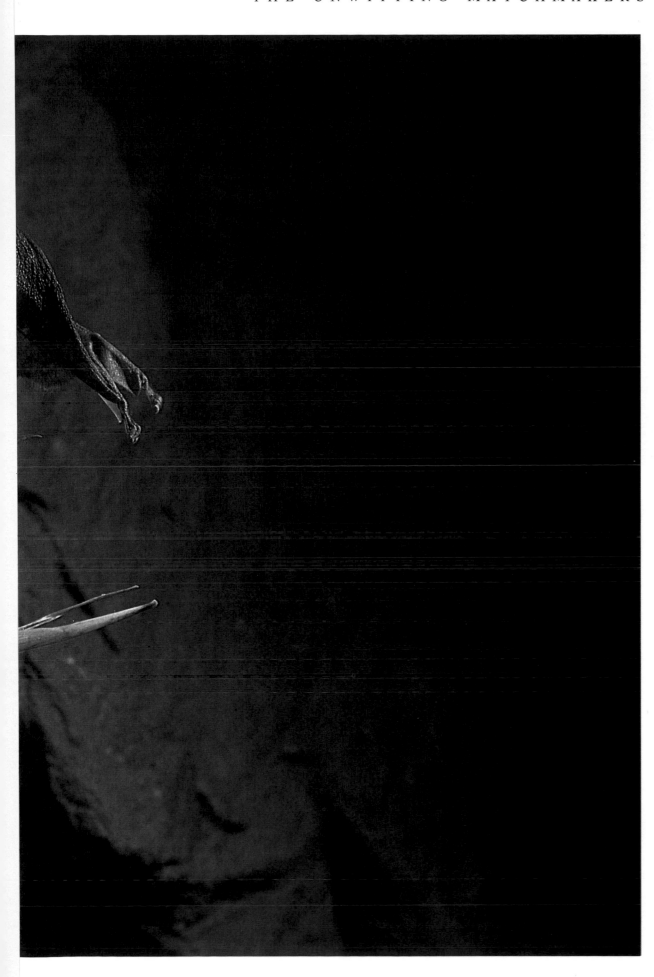

92 GEOFFROY'S LONG-NOSED BAT, SOUTH AMERICA
(Stephen Dalton/NHPA)
MANY RAINFOREST BATS ARE POLLINATORS, WITH MANY FOREST TREES RELYING ON THEM FOR THEIR REPRODUCTION. BATS NAVIGATE AND LOCATE FLOWERS BY SONAR AND CAN VISIT NUMEROUS PLANTS IN ONE NIGHT, PAUSING ONLY A FEW SECONDS AT EACH FLOWER. THE POLLEN IS GENERALLY RUBBED ON TO THE BAT'S FUR AS IT CLINGS MOMENTARILY TO THE FLOWER TO LAP THE NECTAR, BUT SOME BATS, LIKE THIS ONE, HOVER, HUMMINGBIRD-LIKE, OVER THE FLOWER TO SUCK NECTAR WITH THEIR LONG TONGUES.

96

96 'TIGER' BUTTERFLY ON ASCLEPIAS FLOWER, TRINIDAD
(Ken Preston-Mafham/Premaphotos)
THOUGH THIS FLOWER IS FREQUENTLY VISITED BY BUTTERFLIES WHICH FEED ON
THE NECTAR, ITS PRIMARY POLLINATORS ARE WASPS. IN AN ATTEMPT TO GET
SOMETHING FOR NOTHING, A SPECIES OF ORCHID IMITATES THE ASCLEPIAS,
GROWING AMONG IT AND TAKING ADVANTAGE OF ITS POLLINATORS – THOUGH
UNLIKE THE REAL FLOWER IT OFFERS NO NECTAR AS A RETURN FOR THEIR
ATTENTIONS.

97

97 *LANTANA CAMARA* **FLOWER, PERU** (Ken Preston-Mafham/Premaphotos)
WHEREVER IT GROWS THIS FLOWER IS CONSTANTLY ATTENDED BY BUTTERFLIES.
IT IS IDEALLY SHAPED FOR BUTTERFLY FEEDING, PRODUCES COPIOUS NECTAR,
AND GROWS PROFUSELY THROUGHOUT THE TROPICS. ALTHOUGH ITS NATIVE
HOME IS IN SOUTH AMERICA, IT HAS NOW COLONIZED ALL THE CONTINENTS
FROM AFRICA TO ASIA AND AUSTRALIA WHERE, PARTLY AS A RESULT OF THE
BUTTERFLIES' ASSIDUITY IN POLLINATING IT, THE FLOWER HAS BECOME A WEED
AND A PEST.

100 SCARLET MACAW, SOUTH AMERICA (Gerry Ellis/Ellis Wildlife Collection)
ALTHOUGH MANY BIRDS EAT THE FRUITS AND INADVERTENTLY DISPERSE THE
SEEDS THEY CONTAIN, OTHERS ACTUALLY EAT AND DESTROY THE SEEDS. PRIME
AMONG THESE SEED PREDATORS ARE THE PARROTS AND MACAWS, WHICH
REMOVE THE OUTER FLESHY FRUIT COATING WITH THEIR CLAWS AND BEAKS,
THEN CRUNCH THE KERNEL. THE MOUTHPARTS OF THE MACAWS HAVE EVOLVED
TO BE PHENOMENALLY STRONG, AND THEY CAN CRACK EVEN THE HARDEST
SHELLS. MANY SPECIES OF MACAW AND PARROT ARE NOW SERIOUSLY
ENDANGERED, OWING TO THEIR COLLECTION FOR THE WESTERN ANIMAL TRADE

101

101 RESPLENDENT QUETZAL, CLOUD FOREST, COSTA RICA
(Michael and Patricia Fogden)
THE RARE AND BEAUTIFUL QUETZAL, SACRED BIRD OF THE ANCIENT MAYANS, IS
NOW ENDANGERED. THE QUETZAL IS DEPENDENT ON THE WILD AVOCADO
WHICH FORMS A HIGH PROPORTION OF ITS DIET; LIKEWISE, THE AVOCADO
DEPENDS ON THE QUETZAL, WHICH IS ITS PRIMARY DISPERSER. PREVIOUSLY,
QUETZALS WERE NOT VULNERABLE, BUT THE LOSS OF THEIR PRIMARY FOOD
SOURCE TO THE LOGGING COMPANIES (AVOCADOS ARE A FAVOURED TIMBER
TREE), AND SOME POACHING TO MAKE STUFFED BIRDS FOR THE TOURIST TRADE,
HAS NOW SERIOUSLY REDUCED THEIR NUMBERS.

102

102 **TOUCAN, BELIZE** (Simon Zisman/Remote Source)

103 **SAFFRON TOUCANET, SOUTH AMERICA** (Luiz Claudio Marigo)

104 **RHINOCEROS HORNBILL, MALAYSIA** (Morten Strange/NHPA)
CENTRAL AND SOUTH AMERICAN TOUCANS AND TOUCANETS AND THEIR OLD
WORLD EQUIVALENTS, THE HORNBILLS, ARE IMPORTANT DISPERSERS OF FRUIT IN
THE FOREST. THESE BIRDS OFTEN EAT FRUIT WITH QUITE LARGE SEEDS, GAINING
NUTRITION FROM THE JUICY SEED COATING AND SWALLOWING THE
UNDAMAGED SEED WHOLE. BECAUSE MOST BIRDS AIM TO GET RID OF HEAVY
AND NUTRITIONALLY USELESS SEEDS AS SOON AS POSSIBLE, THEY OFTEN
REGURGITATE THEM RATHER THAN PASS THEM OUT IN THEIR DROPPINGS, BUT
SUCH LARGE AND POWERFUL FLIERS AS THESE CAN STILL COVER A
CONSIDERABLE DISTANCE BEFORE DOING SO.

104

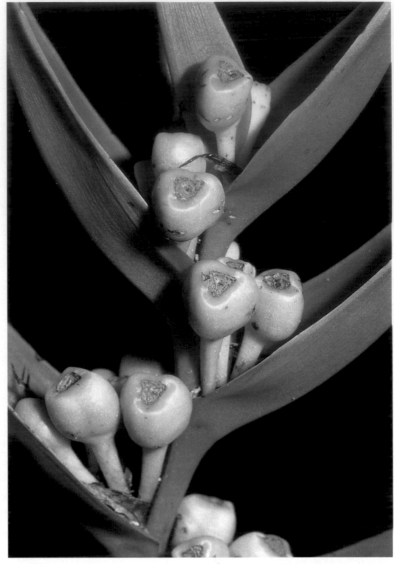

105

105 **HELICONIA FRUIT, VENEZUELA** (Ken Preston-Mafham/Premaphotos)
THE BEAUTIFUL HELICONIA, OR 'LOBSTER-CLAW', FLOWER IS POLLINATED BY
HUMMINGBIRDS AND THEN DEVELOPS SMALL, BERRY-LIKE FRUITS. MOST SPECIES
TEND TO BE DISPERSED BY THE BIRDS WHICH FREQUENT THE UNDERSTOREY
WHERE THESE PLANTS GROW.

106 **PALM FRUIT, SOUTH AMERICA** (Ken Preston-Mafham/Premaphotos)
THE MANY SPECIES OF PALM FRUITS ARE DISPERSED PRIMARILY BY BATS, BIRDS
AND SMALL MAMMALS, WHICH WILL CARRY OFF THOSE WHICH FALL TO THE
GROUND. IN AFRICA, FRUIT BATS ARE NOW REGULARLY BEING SHOT BECAUSE
THEY TAKE VALUABLE FRUITS FROM PLANTATIONS OF THE ECONOMICALLY
IMPORTANT OIL PALM.

146   **MARGAY, BELIZE** (Partridge Films)

147   **JAGUAR PAIR, BELIZE** (Partridge Films)
THE DAPPLED COATS OF THE JUNGLE CATS BLEND PERFECTLY WITH THE LIGHT
ON THE FOREST FLOOR, WHICH SHIFTS AND RIPPLES AS THE FOLIAGE MOVES
ABOVE. UNFORTUNATELY FOR MANY OF THE CATS, PARTICULARLY THE LARGER
JAGUARS AND LEOPARDS, THEIR BEAUTIFUL COATS ARE ALSO DESIRED BY
HUMANS. MANY OF THESE SUPREME RAINFOREST PREDATORS ARE NOW
ENDANGERED THROUGH EXTENSIVE POACHING, WHEN THEY ARE BARBARICALLY

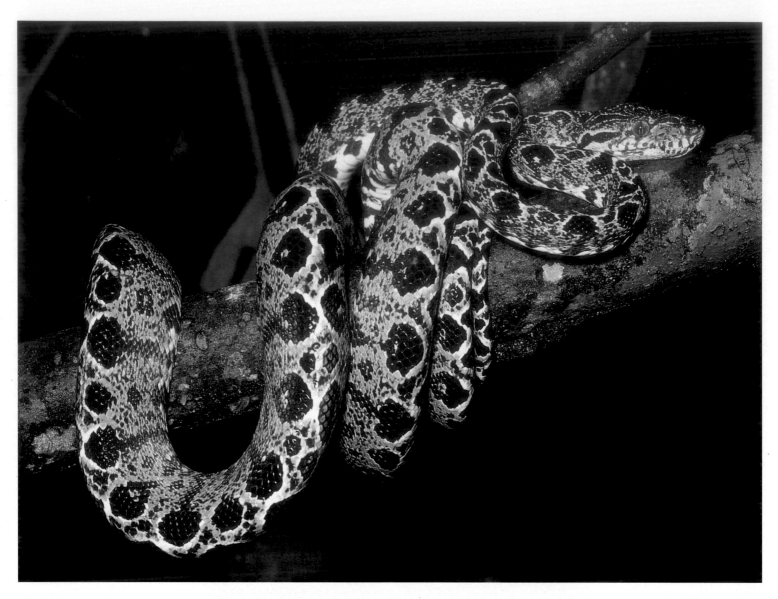

148

148 TREE BOA, ECUADOR
(Michael and Patricia Fogden)
THE POWERFUL TREE BOA
STRANGLES ITS PREY – RODENTS,
BIRDS AND THE LIKE – BY
CONSTRICTING ITS MUSCULAR
COILS. DESPITE ITS STRENGTH IT IS
NOT POISONOUS AND THEREFORE
IS VULNERABLE TO PREDATORS
SUCH AS BIRDS OF PREY.

**149 MOTH CATERPILLAR, COSTA
RICA** (Stephen J Krasemann/NHPA)
THIS HARMLESS CATERPILLAR
CONVINCINGLY MIMICS AN
EXTREMELY POISONOUS VIPER
WITH THE UNDERSIDE OF ITS
BODY, SHOWN HERE. IT IS QUITE
LARGE, SO THE DECEPTION IS
CREDIBLE.

150 PARROT SNAKE, COSTA RICA
(Michael and Patricia Fogden)
A SUPREME BLUFFER, THE PARROT
SNAKE IS NOT VENOMOUS, BUT ITS
VIVID COLOURATION AND
THREATENING POSTURE, WITH
MOUTH GAPING WIDE, IMPLY TO
PREDATORS THAT IT IS.

149

151

151   TURQUOISE ARROW-POISON FROG, CENTRAL AMERICA
(Michael and Patricia Fogden/Bruce Coleman Ltd)
AS ITS NAME SUGGESTS, THE TOXINS IN THIS FROG ARE USED BY
AMERICAN INDIANS TO TIP THEIR ARROWS FOR HUNTING. ALTHOUGH
GREENISH, ITS UNNATURAL, METALLIC COLOURS PROBABLY WARN
PREDATORS OF ITS INEDIBLE NATURE, RATHER THAN CAMOUFLAGING IT.

152   CHAMELEON, MADAGASCAR (Ken Preston-Mafham/Premaphotos)
THE CHAMELEON'S COLORATION DOES NOT, CONTRARY TO MYTH,
CHANGE TO MATCH ITS SURROUNDINGS – THE RESPONSE IS, IN FACT,
TO TEMPERATURE.

153   RED EYED TREE FROG, AUSTRALIA (Ken Preston-Mafham/Premaphotos)
BY NIGHT, THE MALES OF THIS SPECIES GATHER TOGETHER TO
ATTRACT FEMALES BY CALLING IN A LOUD AND RESONANT CHORUS
THROUGH THE FOREST. SUCH MALE COURTING GROUPS ARE KNOWN AS
LEKS AND ARE COMMON AMONG BIRDS, FROGS AND BUTTERFLIES.

152

154

155

CHAPTER SEVEN

BETWEEN THE TREES – THE CANOPY COMMUNITY

ANDREW MITCHELL

*The trees create the framework for the forest, in both
evolutionary and physical terms. Their leaves, fruit and
flowers, even their twigs and resin, support a multitude of
animals, many of which live among their branches high in the
canopy and are never or only rarely seen. More surprisingly,
there are also a whole host of plants which depend on the trees
for their survival - for their access to energy-giving sunlight,
even for their nutrition. These plants in turn are home to a
vast array of smaller animals, inconspicuous beside the bright
birds and the monkeys which dart and leap through the
branches, but which also make up the life of this canopy
community.*

FROM THE DIM FLOOR OF THE RAINFOREST, THE CANOPY
appears as a jungle of interlocking branches and tree limbs
draped with lianas. In fact, it is a complex network of arboreal
highways leading through a maze of spaces, hollows and
niches, providing a wide variety of habitats for the myriad
creatures which inhabit it.

The architecture of individual trees provides the solid matrix
for all other life in the forest. Some, the emergents, grow to tre-
mendous heights. Beneath them nestle other lesser trees which
form the continuous leaf layer of the canopy, and below these
again trees with oblong crowns fit between the massive trunks
of the emergents. Larger animals swing and scamper along
familiar pathways through the canopy with nonchalant ease.

The ability to move with such confidence in the forest is the
product of millions of years of co-evolution between animals
and plants. Many mammals, such as monkeys, have powerful

---

157 **TREE WITH EPIPHYTES, QUEENSLAND, AUSTRALIA** (Leo Meier/Weldon Trannies)
THERE ARE FEW SPACES BETWEEN OR ON THE TREES IN THE RAINFOREST WHICH
ARE NOT COLONIZED. PLANTS HANG AND TWIST AND CLIMB AND CREEP ON
TREES AT EVERY LEVEL FROM FOREST FLOOR TO CANOPY: SOME BENEFIT THE
TREE WHICH IS THEIR HOST, BUT OTHERS SUCK ITS NUTRIENTS, STRANGLE OR
SHADE IT OR WEIGH IT DOWN SO HEAVILY THAT IT DIES. AMONG THE LIANAS
WHICH TRAIL AND THE EPIPHYTIC PLANTS WHICH CLING, ALMOST ROOTLESS, TO
THE TRUNK AND BRANCHES OF THE TREE, LIVE A MULTITUDE OF CREATURES
WHICH MAY NEVER TOUCH THE GROUND.

water. On finding one high above ground she will reverse into it, dropping the tadpoles into the water, each into a separate leaf axil where, safe from ground predators, the tadpoles feed on algae and mosquito larvae. Each day the female returns and reverses again into the bromeliad to touch the water surface. If a tadpole is present it vibrates the water surface with its tail and signals to its mother to release a single unfertilized egg – a food parcel to ensure its survival.

A young canopy tree bound for the forest roof must run the gauntlet of clinging vines and lianas which seek to hitch a ride there too. Some take evasive action: pioneer species which rely on rapid growth to colonize light gaps periodically slough off their bark, perhaps to rid themselves of other hindering plants. Some lianas will outlive the tree in which they grow, rising again into the tree tops on a young tree after their original host has fallen. More remarkable still are the strangling figs. These extraordinary plants begin their life as a tiny seed deposited in the branches of a canopy tree. As the plant grows it sends down roots which on reaching the ground thicken rapidly, sucking moisture and goodness from the earth. Eventually, the strangling fig's branches shade out its host's leaves and encase its trunk in a coffin of roots. Gradually, the host's trunk rots away, leaving a massive hollow lattice of roots belonging to the strangler alone. From such death, new abundance is born because the strangling fig is one of the most prolific fruiting trees in the forest and a whole host of creatures flock to its branches to gorge themselves on figs. This arboreal feast has only one purpose from the fig tree's point of view – to disperse its seeds to fertile places in which new strangling figs may grow. It is no mystery that syrup of figs is a laxative. Fig trees evolved that way to ensure their seeds come through unscathed.

Fortunately, the unusual hollow trunk of the strangling fig confers a benefit which no Darwinian evolutionist could have foreseen. Its numerous tough roots make the mature tree difficult and dangerous to fell even with a chainsaw, bulldozer or axe. After loggers have passed, the *Matapalo*, or death-tree as the strangling fig is sometimes known, is often the only species left standing, a forlorn island of hope for the forest's survivors, in a wasteland of fallen trees.

158 TIJUCA FOREST, BRAZIL (Susan L Cunningham)
THE LIANAS ARE WOODY CLIMBERS WHICH ARE ABUNDANT IN RAINFOREST, WHERE THEY MAY ACCOUNT FOR EIGHT PER CENT OF THE TOTAL SPECIES. THEIR TEMPERATE EQUIVALENTS ARE FAMILIAR GARDEN PLANTS SUCH AS IVY, CLEMATIS AND WOODBINE. IN THE TROPICS, THEY GROW TO ENORMOUS SIZES: 15 M/50 FT DIAMETER IS NOT EXCEPTIONAL AND A RATTAN CLIMBER WAS ONCE MEASURED AT 165 M/180 YDS LONG. OFTEN THEY WILL OUTLIVE THE TREE WHICH ORIGINALLY SUPPORTED THEM. IT IS NOT UNUSUAL IN THE FOREST TO SEE GREAT WOODY LASSOS DANGLING FROM THE CANOPY ABOVE, AN EMPTY LOOP WHERE ONCE THERE WAS A TREE. ALTHOUGH SOME LIANAS THRIVE IN DISTURBED FOREST WHERE THERE IS MORE LIGHT, OTHERS WILL ONLY GROW IN PRIMARY FOREST.

159 **BROMELIADS GROWING ON TREE, BRAZIL** (Luiz Claudio Marigo) PLANTS OF THE BROMELIAD FAMILY, WHICH WE FREQUENTLY SEE AS HOUSEPLANTS, OFTEN GROW AS EPIPHYTES IN THE COOL AND ULTRA-HUMID MONTANE FORESTS OF SOUTH AMERICA. EPIPHYTES ARE PLANTS WHICH HAVE GAINED ACCESS TO THE SUN WITHOUT HAVING TO EXPEND ENERGY BY GROWING TRUNKS, STEMS OR ROOTS WHICH TAP INTO THE GROUND. INSTEAD, THEIR SEEDS LODGE IN CREVICES AND CRACKS HIGH IN A TREE AND THERE THEY GROW, SUCKING MOISTURE AND NUTRIENT PARTICLES FROM THE AIR, SOMETIMES STEALING NOURISHMENT FROM THEIR HOST PLANT OR GATHERING FOREST DEBRIS AMONG THEIR LEAVES FOR THEIR OWN FOOD STORE.

159

160

160 RED-BILLED SCYTHE BILL, BRAZIL (Luiz Claudio Marigo) THIS SCYTHE BILL IS, LIKE THE HUMMINGBIRDS, A NECTAR FEEDER. DARTING AMONG THE TREES, IT FREQUENTLY FEEDS ON THE NECTAR OF THE BRIGHTLY COLOURED BROMELIAD FLOWERS, WHICH SHINE LIKE BEACONS AMONG THE DENSE FOREST FOLIAGE.

161 BROMELIADS AND OTHER EPIPHYTES, BLUE MOUNTAINS, JAMAICA (Michael and Patricia Fogden) HIGH IN THE CANOPY, THE ROTTING LEAVES AND INSECTS TRAPPED BY THE LEAVES OF BROAD SPIKY EPIPHYTES, PARTICULARLY BROMELIADS, CAN BECOME A USEFUL SOURCE OF NUTRITION FOR THE HOST TREE. SOME GROW ROOTS INTO 'THEIR' EPIPHYTES, PIRATING THE GATHERED NUTRIENTS FOR THEIR OWN BENEFIT.

161

162

163

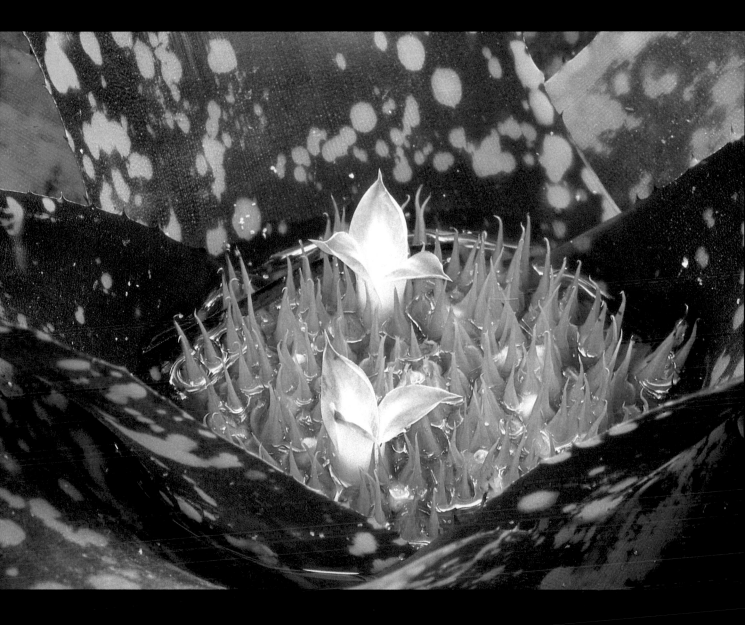

162   BROMELIAD, SOUTH AMERICA (James Carmichael/NHPA)

163   ORANGE STAR BROMELIAD, SOUTH AMERICA
(Gerry Ellis/Ellis Wildlife Collection)

164   *NEOREGELIA INCA* BROMELIAD, DOMINICAN REPUBLIC
(Gerry Ellis/Ellis Wildlife Collection)

165   HAGENIA TREES, RWANDA (Gerry Ellis/Ellis Wildlife Collection)
PLANTS OTHER THAN BROMELIADS THAT GROW ON TREES INCLUDE ARBOREAL

166 MYRMECODIA EPIPHYTE, ARU ISLAND (Alain Compost/Bruce Coleman Ltd)
THIS EPIPHYTE IS COLONIZED BY TINY ANTS, WHICH BY NIGHT SCOUR THE
FOREST FLOOR FOR INSECT CORPSES WHICH THEY THEN CARRY BACK TO THEIR
ARBOREAL NEST. THE DEAD INSECTS ARE STORED AND USED AS COMPOST FOR
THE ANTS' 'FUNGUS GARDENS' WHICH THEY CULTIVATE WITHIN THE EPIPHYTE.
THE ANTS FEED ON THE FUNGI WHILE THE EPIPHYTE USES NUTRIENTS RELEASED
BY THE FUNGAL GROWTH.

167 PYGMY MARSUPIAL FROG,
CENTRAL AMERICA

(Michael Fogden/Bruce Coleman Ltd)

THESE TINY MARSUPIAL FROGS ARE
RELATIVELY EASY TO FIND SITTING
AMONG THE LEAVES. THIS FEMALE
HAS HAD HER FERTLIZED EGGS
PLACED IN THE SAC UNDER THE
SKIN ON HER BACK BY HER MATE
WHERE THEY WILL MATURE, TO
TADPOLE STAGE. AT THIS POINT
SHE TIPS THEM INTO A WATER
POOL TO FINISH THEIR
DEVELOPMENT.

167

168 RED AND BLUE POISON-
ARROW FROG

(Michael Fogden/Bruce Coleman Ltd)

169 RETICULATED POISON-ARROW
FROG, PERU

(Michael and Patricia Fogden)

MANY OF THE POISON-ARROW
FROGS LAY THEIR EGGS ON LAND,
AFTER WHICH THE EGGS ARE
GUARDED, USUALLY BY THE MALE
BUT SOMETIMES BY THE FEMALE,
UNTIL THEY HATCH. THE NEW
TADPOLES THEN WRIGGLE ONTO
THE BACK OF THE FEMALE, WHO
BEGINS A LONG CLIMB INTO THE
CANOPY. HER MISSION IS TO FIND A
BROMELIAD FILLED WITH WATER,
INTO WHICH SHE CAREFULLY
DROPS EACH TADPOLE. THE
TADPOLES WILL MATURE INTO
FROGS IN THE BROMELIAD POOL,
NURTURED BY THE MOTHER, WHO
CONTINUES TO PROVIDE FOOD FOR
THEM ON DAILY VISITS.

168

169

170 RED-EYED LEAF FROGS, COSTA
RICA (Michael and Patricia Fogden)
RED-EYED LEAF FROGS, OR GAUDY
FROGS AS THEY ARE ALSO,
UNDERSTANDABLY, KNOWN, SPEND
MANY OF THE DAYTIME HOURS IN
BROMELIAD POOLS OR SITTING ON
A GREEN LEAF. BREEDING TAKES
PLACE BY NIGHT, BEGINNING WHEN
THE FEMALE ANSWERS A 'CLUCK'
FROM A NEARBY MALE. SHE MAY
LAY SEVERAL CLUTCHES OF EGGS
IN ONE NIGHT. SHOWN HERE IS
THE MALE MATING WITH THE
MUCH LARGER FEMALE; BUT A
SECOND MALE (SEEN ABOVE) IS
TRYING TO CLAIM THE RIGHT
AS HIS.

175 RED COLOBUS, GAMBIA
(Stephen Dalton/NHPA)

176 BLACK SPIDER MONKEY, PERU
(Gunter Ziesler/Bruce Coleman Ltd)
FOR THE AGILE MONKEYS OF THE
CANOPY, THE INTERLOCKED TREES
AND MESHED LIANAS WAY ABOVE
THE GROUND FORM WELL-KNOWN
PATHWAYS WHICH ARE IN
CONSTANT USE. THERE IS LITTLE
NEED FOR EITHER OF THESE
MONKEYS EVER TO DESCEND TO
THE FOREST FLOOR. SPIDER
MONKEYS ARE INCREDIBLY
RELAXED IN THE TREE TOPS: AGILE
AND MOBILE, THEY USE THEIR
TAILS AS A FIFTH LIMB WHICH
PERMITS ENDLESS VARIATION OF
MOVEMENT. THE LARGE RED
COLOBUS IS ALSO A FOREST
ACROBAT CAPABLE OF
SPECTACULAR LEAPS, BUT IS FAR
LESS ENERGETIC THAN THE SPIDER
MONKEY. THE REASON LIES IN THE
RESPECTIVE DIGESTIVE SYSTEMS
OF THE SPECIES: THE SPIDER
MONKEY EATS ENERGY-RICH,
EASILY DIGESTED FRUIT, WHEREAS
THE COLOBUS EATS ALMOST
EXCLUSIVELY LEAVES. THESE IT
DIGESTS IN A DOUBLE STOMACH,
RATHER LIKE AN AERIAL COW:
SUCH DIGESTION TAKES TIME.
HENCE THE COLOBUS' LAZIER
LIFESTYLE.

175

176

177 RUFOUS MOUSE LEMUR,
MADAGASCAR
(Ken Preston-Mafham/Premaphotos)
AMONG THE SMALLEST OF ALL THE
PRIMATES, THE MOUSE LEMUR
SCURRIES THROUGH THE TREES
WITH SOME AGILITY. BY DAY,
GROUPS OF UP TO FIFTEEN
FEMALES AND YOUNG LEMURS
SLEEP IN NESTS BUILT IN DENSE
FOLIAGE OR IN HOLES IN TREES; BY
NIGHT THEY DISPERSE TO FORAGE,
PARTICULARLY FOR FRUIT.

179

179 PITCHER PLANT, MADAGASCAR

(O. Langrand/Bruce Coleman Ltd)
PITCHERS ARE AMONG THE
RELATIVELY FEW CARNIVOROUS
PLANTS IN THE WORLD: THEY TRAP,
DROWN AND DIGEST INSECTS IN
THEIR LIQUID-FILLED PITCHERS.
MANY CARNIVOROUS INSECTS ALSO
EXPLOIT THE PITCHER'S ABILITIES,
AND FEED ON THE DEAD AND
DYING INSECTS: TWENTY-SEVEN
SPECIES WERE RECORDED IN ONE
KIND OF PITCHER. ALTHOUGH
USUALLY A PLANT OF SOUTH-EAST
ASIAN FORESTS, THIS SPECIES IS
ENDEMIC TO MADAGASCAR.

178

**178 CLIMBING PEPPER VINE,
BORNEO**

(Ken Preston-Mafham/Premaphotos)
NON-WOODY CLIMBING PLANTS
SUCH AS THIS PEPPER ARE
COMMON IN THE FOREST,
PARTICULARLY IN MORE OPEN
AREAS WITH PLENTY OF LIGHT,
WHERE THE VINES CAN FORM A
VERITABLE BLANKET OVER THE
VEGETATION. LIKE ALL THE
CLIMBERS AND THE EPIPHYTES,
THEIR GAIN IS THAT THEY SAVE
ENERGY BY RELYING ON ANOTHER
PLANT FOR SUPPORT.

180

180   STRANGLING FIG: QUEENSLAND, AUSTRALIA (Kathie Atkinson/OSF)
STRANGLING FIGS GROW IN TROPICAL FORESTS ALL OVER THE WORLD, STARTING
AS TINY SEEDS LODGED IN THE RAINFOREST CANOPY. THE TINY PLANT GROWS
ON ITS HOST UNTIL IT IS LARGE ENOUGH TO SEND DOWN LONG ROOTS TO THE
GROUND, WHERE THEY SUCK UP NUTRIENTS AND WATER. THE ROOTS THICKEN
AND SOLIDIFY, EVENTUALLY BECOMING TRUNK-LIKE IN SIZE. BY THIS TIME THE
FIG HAS ABSORBED THE NUTRIENTS DESTINED FOR THE ORIGINAL TREE AND
SHADED IT FROM THE SUN IT NEEDS FOR GROWTH; THE TREE DIES AND FINALLY
ROTS AWAY, LEAVING A HOLLOW FIG TREE WHOSE TRUNK IS A NETWORK OF
ENORMOUS WOODY ROOTS.

CHAPTER EIGHT

FROM DEATH INTO LIFE –
THE NEVERENDING CYCLE
Professor David Bellamy

In the rainforest more than in any other environment, death is the source of new life. Dead leaves, wood, flowers and insects fall in a continuous rain from the trees, littering the forest floor; occasionally the body of a larger animal is also seen. But nothing lies there for long: every scrap of debris is rapidly processed by a multitude of micro-organisms, plants and animals known as the decomposers. These feed on the dead matter, breaking it down so that ultimately almost every one of its useful molecules is made available for use by the green plants which are the basis of life in the forest. This highly efficient system of recycling helps to explain the luxuriance of tropical forests: for the paradox is that its abundant growth rests, in nearly every case, on soils which are acid and poor in nutrients.

RAINFORESTS ARE BY DEFINITION DOMINATED BY trees, each one of which is a sophisticated chemical factory, combining the energy of the sun, the rainwater that gives the forests their name, and carbon dioxide from the atmosphere in the process of photosynthesis. The product is energy – essential for fuelling the trees' growth, and for the manufacture of a whole gamut of complex biochemicals – sugars, amino acids, proteins, cellulose, tannins, lignins, fats, waxes, hormones, drugs and fragrances, to name but a few. Many a multinational company would be proud to list such a range on their catalogues – but no industrial complex yet designed by humans could produce anything like such a variety and number of biochemical products using so few resources, on such economically arranged premises, and with no harmful wastes or by-products.

It must be admitted, however, that trees are the world's number one litter louts, for there is really no such thing as a truly

---

do not photosynthesize but feed by digesting dead organic matter with special enzymes, and in the process release nutrients for use by other plants. Particularly essential to the ecosystem are the mycorrhizal fungi, which weave their threads into a mat around and even inside the roots of the canopy trees, feeding from the sugar and nitrogen containing substances within. In return, the roots take up from the fungi the minerals it has absorbed from the debris of the forest. Thus the greatest and the least of the forest's plants are linked in a symbiotic association which from death and decay produces fresh growth and new life.

So the continuous rain of death from above – leaves, twigs and flowers – along with the carcasses of animals great and small are transformed by the decomposers into components which can be reused by the green plants, the base of the forest food chain. There is no room for waste, for if the cycle of the rainforest is broken, the precious minerals will leach out and the rain will carry them away. The living soil, already sour and impoverished, will no longer be able to support all the wonder of the forest.

Thus the rainforest recycles itself, making no demands on the rest of the environment. Yet its every hectare contributes to the rest of the world, both in terms of the materials it provides and by performing a vital function within the balance of nature: and the most remarkable thing is that in its natural state it costs not one penny piece, not a single calorie of fossil or atomic fuel, nor gramme of non-renewable resource to maintain.

Nevertheless, one million hectares are being destroyed each month: a million hectares of the system which gives life to at least half of all the sorts of plants and animals on earth. At the present rate of destruction, within forty years there will be no large areas left. Climates are changing, deserts are expanding, and already people are suffering. By the end of this sad century more than one million rainforest species will have been forced into extinction and one third of all the world's arable and pastoral land will have become semi-desert. The global consequences of rainforest destruction are far more terrible in their implications even than a limited atomic war. This destruction must be stopped now before it is too late.

---

182 SNAIL ON BAMBOO, PUERTO RICO (Gerry Ellis/Ellis Wildlife Collection)
PLANTS CONTAIN BASIC NUTRIENTS, SOME OF WHICH CANNOT BE
MANUFACTURED BY ANIMALS. HERBIVOROUS ANIMALS RELY ON PLANTS FIRST TO
PROCESS THE NUTRIENTS, WHICH THEY THEN ABSORB 'SECOND HAND', READY-
CONVERTED FOR THEIR USE. THESE HERBIVORES ARE THEN EATEN IN THEIR
TURN BY THE CARNIVORES. THUS THE NUTRIENTS ARE IN ACTIVE SERVICE ALL
ALONG THE FOOD CHAIN, FROM THE TINIEST SEEDLING TO THE LARGEST
CARNIVORE.

183

183   LEAF-CUTTER ANTS, COSTA RICA (Ken Preston-Mafham/Premaphotos)
LEAF-CUTTER ANTS, COMMON THROUGHOUT TROPICAL AMERICA, BREAK DOWN
HUGE AMOUNTS OF VEGETATION. THE PIECES OF LEAVES – AND SOMETIMES
FLOWERS – ARE TAKEN BACK TO THEIR UNDERGROUND NESTS, WHERE THEY ARE
FURTHER SHREDDED AND PROCESSED BY WORKERS, AND FINALLY SOWN WITH
FUNGAL SPORES. THE RESULTING FUNGUS GARDENS PROVIDE THE ANTS WITH
FOOD.

184   LEAF SKELETON ON LIVERWORT, PUERTO RICO (Gerry Ellis/Ellis Wildlife Collection)

185   CRABCLAW TREE BLOSSOMS, PUERTO RICO (Gerry Ellis/Ellis Wildlife Collection)

186   LEAVES IN WATER, AUSTRALIA (Leo Meier/Weldon Trannies)

187   POINSETTIA LEAVES, PUERTO RICO (Gerry Ellis)
EACH LEAF WHICH DROPS TO THE GROUND IN THE RAINFOREST BECOMES PART
OF THE LEAF LITTER, A THIN LAYER OF ORGANIC MATERIAL IN VARYING STAGES
OF DECOMPOSITION. THESE LEAVES WILL SOON BE UNRECOGNIZABLE: THE RATE
OF PRODUCTION IN THE FOREST, FUELLED BY LIGHT, HEAT AND DAMP, IS
ENORMOUSLY FAST. IT IS KEPT IN DYNAMIC BALANCE BY AN EQUALLY
PRODIGIOUS RATE OF DECOMPOSITION.

184

185

186

187

191   PARASOL FUNGUS, COSTA RICA (Michael and Patricia Fogden)
THESE TINY PARASOLS MEASURE ONLY 6MM/¼IN ACROSS. DAVID BELLAMY SAW
THEM USED BY THE AUKA INDIANS OF THE AMAZON FOREST TO CURE
DIARRHOEA IN INFANTS. A PASTE MADE FROM THE FUNGI WAS SPREAD ON THE
MOTHER'S BREAST AND FED TO HER BABY, WITH IMPRESSIVE RESULTS.

194

193

195

193   STINKHORN, UNDESCRIBED SPECIES, COSTA RICA (Michael and Patricia Fogden)

194   FUNGUS IN CLOUD FOREST, EAST AFRICA (Peter Ward/Bruce Coleman Ltd)

195   FUNGUS, SABAH (Ivan Polunin/NHPA)

FUNGI PRODUCE REPRODUCTIVE SPORES WHICH NEED TO BE DISPERSED AND,
LIKE MANY GREEN PLANTS, THEY SOMETIMES ENLIST THE HELP OF INSECTS. THE
STINKHORN PRODUCES AN UNPLEASANT-SMELLING LIQUID ATTRACTIVE TO FLIES,
WHICH COLLECT SPORES ON THEIR FEET TO SCATTER ELSEWHERE; OTHER FUNGI
EXPLODE, SCATTERING THEIR DUST-LIKE SPORES AROUND THEM. STILL OTHERS
IMPREGNATE INSECTS WHICH MOVE ON AND THEN DIE, PROVIDING NUTRITION
FOR THE FUNGI WHICH GROW FROM THEIR BODIES AND WHICH THEN SCATTER
THEIR SPORES ONTO YET MORE UNWITTING INSECTS.

196

196   TERMITE WORKERS HARVESTING DEAD LEAVES, MALAYSIA
(Ken Preston-Mafham/Premaphotos)
THERE ARE ABOUT 2000 SPECIES OF TERMITES THROUGHOUT THE FORESTS OF
THE WORLD, ALL SHYING AWAY FROM LIGHT AND DROUGHT, LIVING IN
ELABORATE MUD MOUNDS OR UNDERGROUND NESTS. THEY ARE IMPORTANT
DECOMPOSERS OF PLANT MATTER, CLEANING THE FOREST BY VORACIOUSLY
FEEDING ON DEAD WOOD DIGESTED WITH THE HELP OF MICRO-ORGANISMS
LIVING IN THEIR GUT.

197

197 NYMPHALID BUTTERFLY FEEDING ON DUNG, PERU

(Ken Preston-Mafham/Premaphotos
MANY BUTTERFLIES FEED ON ANIMAL WASTE SUCH AS URINE AND DUNG, SUPPLEMENTING THE SALT WHICH IS LOST IN SPERM PRODUCTION IN PARTICULAR. THEY, TOO, HELP TO RECYCLE NUTRIENTS WHICH MIGHT OTHERWISE BE DISSOLVED BY THE RAIN AND LOST.

198 FORAGING ARMY ANTS, TRINIDAD

(David Thompson/OSF)
RAINFOREST ANTS ARE CARRION-EATERS AS WELL AS BEING PREDATORS OF LIVING INSECTS. THEY CAN QUICKLY DISMEMBER ANY CARCASS THEY FIND ON THE FOREST FLOOR. THE HOOK-LIKE JAWS OF THESE ARMY ANTS ARE SO STRONG THAT THEY WERE USED BY AMERICAN INDIANS TO 'STITCH' WOUNDS: THE ANT WAS MADE TO BITE EITHER SIDE OF THE CUT, DRAWING THE SKIN TOGETHER; ITS BODY WAS THEN REMOVED, LEAVING ONLY THE JAWS.

198

CHAPTER NINE

PEOPLE OF THE FOREST
ROBIN HANBURY-TENISON

If you damage your environment, it will no longer support your needs. This simple but essential rule is unwittingly complied with by all the creatures of the animal kingdom. Ironically, the human race all too often ignores it. The consequences can be dire. But in many of the ancient tropical rainforests live people who do understand the imperative of maintaining the finely balanced ecosystem on which they depend for all they need. Over the millennia, forest peoples have found ever more sophisticated methods of simultaneously exploiting and managing their environment, acknowledging their debt to the land in a multitude of ways. We might well follow their example, and learn from their great expertise: but the chances of doing so are fast disappearing. For the people of the rainforest, discounted and exploited in the race for financial gain, are losing their cultural identities, their freedom and even their lives with every acre of forest destroyed.

T HE RAINFORESTS WERE ALREADY MANY MILLIONS OF years old when the first hunter-gatherers ventured into their vast and unknown interior. The forests of South East Asia were the first to be colonized, some forty thousand years ago; much later, people also entered those of America and Africa. Travelling nomadically, the ancestral pioneers probably carried few possessions besides their intelligence and resourcefulness. As they migrated ever deeper into the forest, they began to discover how best to extract a living from the world which towered around them.

Since those first hunter-gatherers began to learn which fruits were the sweetest and which game the best, which vines healed wounds and which yielded lethal arrow poison, such forest lore

---

199 CHIEF RAONI, BRAZIL (Bill Leimbach/South American Pictures)
RAONI, A CHIEF OF THE KAYAPO INDIANS IN XINGU, BRAZIL, HAS BECOME A SYMBOL OF THE WORLDWIDE STRUGGLE TO SAVE THE TROPICAL RAINFORESTS. FOR THOUSANDS OF YEARS, RAONI'S ANCESTORS HAVE LIVED IN THE FOREST; IT HAS SUPPLIED THEIR EVERY NEED AND HAS, IN RETURN, BEEN TREATED WITH GREAT REVERENCE. TODAY, HIS PEOPLE SEE HUGE TRACTS OF THEIR TERRITORY QUITE LITERALLY GOING UP IN SMOKE TO MAKE WAY FOR RANCHING, MINING, AND FARMING: SUCH AREAS WILL PROBABLY NEVER AGAIN BE ABLE TO SUPPORT RAINFOREST GROWTH. WITH THE LOSS OF THEIR LANDS, FOREST PEOPLE EVERYWHERE ARE LOSING THEIR VERY MEANS OF SURVIVAL, ALONG WITH THEIR EXTRAORDINARY CULTURES, REFINED OVER THE MILLENNIA TO ENABLE THEM TO LIVE IN BALANCE WITH THE MOST COMPLEX NATURAL ENVIRONMENTS ON EARTH.

baskets, drawing on each area they pass through for what it can offer: game, fish, mushrooms, yams, fruits or insects.

Superbly skilful in the ways of the forest, the Baka 'read' the signs which will lead them to find food: a few faint tracks, a mound of half-eaten fruits, the shaking of leaves in the treetops, the call of a certain bird or the flowering of a certain tree. They can tell, for instance, by the flight path of a bee or even its buzzing high in the canopy where its nest is located: later they will scale the tree, despite its dizzying height, to plunder the nest for the honeycombs it contains.

As they move through the forest, the Baka build small hunting camps, clearing a small area but leaving the large trees – for, environmental considerations aside, these would take hours to fell. The women weave igloo-shaped huts from pliable saplings and thatch them with large leaves, until they become organic mounds in the shifting, dappled light of the understorey. At night, there may be a dance or a story by firelight, designed for entertainment but also to celebrate the forest and weaken the animals for the hunters. After a few days, the group moves on. A week later, tendrils curl around the huts of the abandoned camp; on occasion the sapling frameworks actually root and produce new green shoots.

The Baka are motivated to begin their long forest trips by the onset of the rainy season, for this heralds the fruiting of the wild mango trees. Wild mangoes are valued not only for their juicy flesh, but also for the oil-yielding kernel they contain: animals seek out the fruits as well, so game is plentiful and easy to track in the damp ground. An awareness of the seasons and moods of the forest, and how they influence its plants and animals, is central to the lives of such people, allowing them to exploit their environment with supreme efficiency. The Yanomami, for instance, collect more than five hundred different wild plants, as well as fruit, fish, frogs and even insects such as caterpillars and termites at different times during the forest cycle, and their meals are seldom identical on two consecutive days throughout the year.

Among all the diverse life of the forest, only people are able to access every part of their environment – even turning its defences to their own advantage. The early hunter-gatherers must have been avid and adventurous experimenters, for today their descendants know the individual properties of literally thousands of plants: in many varied and extraordinary ways they exploit the chemistry of the forest, often the very chemicals designed by plants to protect themselves from predators. Over the generations, plants have been found to dull pain, heal wounds, cure fever, induce visions, reduce or increase fertility, stimulate or tranquillise; poisons have been found which kill fish or game but are harmless when taken by mouth.

A meagre one per cent of tropical rainforest plants have been investigated by Western scientists for their potential. This is thrown into perspective when we remember that some forty per cent of prescribed drugs have a (mainly tropical) plant origin. Although scientists began to take tribal healers seriously only very recently, many drug-yielding plants were only 'discovered' because of their place in traditional medicine. The dainty, pink-flowered Rosy Periwinkle of Madagascar had been used by forest people for generations: in 1960 its properties were finally investigated. Then, four out of every five children with leukaemia died; today, with drugs derived from the Rosy Periwinkle, the same number now survive.

There are many more examples. Quinine, the first effective and widely used treatment for malaria, is derived from the bark of the South American Chinchona tree. It has now been largely replaced by synthetic drugs, but in the wake of increasing resistance by the malaria parasite to these treatments, scientists are once more turning to the 'fever bark' tree for inspiration. The contraceptive pill is derived from a Mexican yam: many other natural contraceptives (and abortives) are used by forest people. Curare, with which the Amazonian Indians poison-tip their arrows, is the basis of a muscle relaxant now used extensively in Western surgery; while the cardiac glycosides of African Strophanthus vine seeds, also used in making arrow poison, are stimulants which are now used in the treatment of heart disease.

The list goes in, but the important point is that plants, particularly rainforest plants, are sources of an immense range of chemicals. Their uninvestigated potential could yield a still greater range of medicines, not to mention other useful substances – foods, perfumes, insecticides, dyes, waxes, fuels, oils, and hundreds more. Forest people, by definition, know their individual properties better than anyone: but with every acre of forest that is destroyed, the possibilities for new discoveries are reduced. This is partly because the plants themselves are being lost – it has been estimated that one animal or plant becomes extinct every half hour because of environmental abuse – but more particularly because the traditional, unwritten knowledge of forest people is itself rapidly disappearing. The forest people are losing their knowledge along with their culture; and they are losing their culture mainly because its source, the forest, is disappearing.

Knowledge, however, may be the very least of their losses as their world is flattened around them. For the peoples of the forest, the devastation of their homeland spells rapid cultural degeneration, despair and often the death of the whole tribe. In Brazil alone one tribe has become extinct every year since the turn of the century.

Only in this century have other humans appeared in great numbers in the rainforest: but they are destroying it at such a prodigious rate that if they continue, within forty years only isolated pockets of forest will be left. The traditional forest

201   **ORANG ASLI VILLAGE, PENINSULAR MALAYSIA** (Neil Gale)

202   **BAKA PYGMY VILLAGE, CAMEROON** (Phil Agland/Dja River Films)

203   **OROKO VILLAGE, CAMEROON** (Edward Parker/Hutchison Library)
SINCE THEY FIRST COLONIZED THE RAINFORESTS THOUSANDS OF YEARS AGO,
PEOPLE HAVE FOUND WAYS OF EXTRACTING EVERYTHING THEY NEED FROM
THEIR ENVIRONMENT; BUT, RECOGNIZING THAT IT IS THE KEY TO THEIR
SURVIVAL, THEY HAVE EVOLVED WAYS OF EXPLOITING IT WITHOUT HARMING IT.
EVEN THESE VILLAGE CLEARINGS ARE SMALL ENOUGH TO BE QUICKLY
RECLAIMED BY THE TREES WHEN THE INHABITANTS SHIFT SITES, WHICH THEY
WILL PROBABLY DO AFTER A FEW YEARS. WE COULD LEARN MUCH ABOUT THE
SUSTAINABLE USE OF THE ENVIRONMENT FROM SUCH PEOPLE, IF ONLY THEY
AND THEIR LAND ARE ALLOWED TO SURVIVE.

204 YANOMAMI INDIANS, BRAZIL
(Robin Hanbury-Tenison/Robert Harding
Picture Library)
RAINFOREST COMMUNITIES TEND
TO BE SMALL, WHICH BOTH
ENSURES THAT THERE ARE
ENOUGH OF THE FOREST'S
RELATIVELY SCARCE RESOURCES
TO GO ROUND, AND THAT THE
IMPACT OF EACH GROUP ON THE
ENVIRONMENT IS MINIMAL. WHOLE
VILLAGES ARE OFTEN MADE UP OF
A SINGLE MUCH EXTENDED
FAMILY, WHICH ENCOURAGES
HARMONY BETWEEN INDIVIDUALS.
THIS IS IMPORTANT, AS MANY SUCH
SOCIETIES RELY HEAVILY ON
COOPERATION BETWEEN THEIR
MEMBERS. ESSENTIAL JOBS LIKE
HUNTING, GATHERING, FOOD
PREPARATION AND SO ON ALL
TEND TO BE SHARED, THOUGH AS
MUCH FOR THE SAKE OF
COMPANIONSHIP AS EFFICIENCY.

205

205   YANOMAMI SHAMAN PREPARING HALLUCINOGENIC SNUFF, BRAZIL
(Robin Hanbury-Tenison/Robert Harding Picture Library)
MOST TRADITIONAL RAINFOREST SOCIETIES IDENTIFY THOUSANDS OF USEFUL
PLANTS, MANY OF WHICH MAY BE USED FOR MEDICAL OR RITUAL PURPOSES. THE
SHAMAN, THE MYSTIC HEALER OF INDIAN SOCIETIES, IS SEEN HERE PREPARING
HALLUCINOGENIC SNUFF FROM THE BARK OF THE VIROLA TREE WHICH WILL
ENABLE HIM TO COMMUNICATE WITH THE YANOMAMI SPIRIT WORLD. IT IS
LIKELY THAT SUCH DRUGS COULD PROVE USEFUL IN TREATING PSYCHOLOGICAL
AND STRESS-RELATED DISORDERS, BUT UNTIL RECENTLY SO LITTLE CREDIT HAS
BEEN GIVEN TO TRADITIONAL MEDICINES THAT VIRTUALLY NONE HAVE BEEN
SCIENTIFICALLY INVESTIGATED. SOME THAT HAVE BEEN ARE NOW USED IN THE
WEST, AND MANY SAVE LIVES. THE FOREST PEOPLE'S KNOWLEDGE COULD REVEAL
THOUSANDS MORE REVOLUTIONARY DRUGS FROM SOURCES AS YET UNKNOWN
TO THE REST OF THE WORLD.

206

206 HEALING WITH FIRE AMONG THE BAKA PYGMIES, CAMEROON (Lisa Silcock/Dja River Films)

207

207 MOTHER AND FATHER MOURNING DEAD SON, PAPUA NEW GUINEA (Maureen Mackenzie/Robert Harding Picture Library) THE OVERLAP BETWEEN THE PHYSICAL AND THE PSYCHOLOGICAL AND SPIRITUAL IS GENERALLY FAR GREATER IN TRADITIONAL SOCIETIES THAN IN OUR OWN. ILLNESS MAY OFTEN BE ATTRIBUTED TO BAD SPIRITS OR ILL-WISHERS; HENCE THE USE OF MAGIC AND RITUAL – AS IN THE FIRE CEREMONY (206) – TO HEAL. AN AWARENESS OF THE SPIRIT WORLD IS EXTREMELY IMPORTANT: A DEATH IS OFTEN ACCOMPANIED BY SPECIFIC MOURNING RITUALS, WHICH ARE DESIGNED TO APPEASE THE SPIRIT OF THE DECEASED, ENSURING THAT IT RESTS QUIETLY AND DOES NOT DISTURB THE LIVING.

208

**208 YANOMAMI WOMEN
COLLECTING FIREWOOD, BRAZIL**
(Robin Hanbury-Tenison/Robert Harding
Picture Library)
IT MAY SEEM NO DIFFICULT TASK
TO COLLECT FIREWOOD WHEN YOU
ARE SURROUNDED BY TREES, BUT
EVEN IN SUCH SIMPLE JOBS, AS IN
ALL ASPECTS OF FOREST LIFE,
SOME SPECIALIZED KNOWLEDGE IS
NEEDED, WHICH COMES FROM
LESSONS LEARNED IN CHILDHOOD.
SOME WOODS BURN THROUGH THE
NIGHT, OTHERS FLARE AND
QUICKLY DIE; WHILE DAMP WOOD
AND NEW WOOD DO NOT BURN AT
ALL.

209

210

209 CLIMBING FOR HONEY, CAMEROON (Lisa Silcock/Dja River Films)

210 A HAUL OF WILD HONEYCOMBS, CAMEROON (Lisa Silcock/Dja River Films)
FOR THE BAKA PYGMIES OF CAMEROON, HONEY IS THE MOST PRIZED FOOD OF
ALL; THEY COLLECT IT FROM SEVENTEEN DIFFERENT KINDS OF BEE USING A
VARIETY OF TECHNIQUES. THE AFRICAN HONEYBEE NESTS HIGH IN THE CANOPY.
A SKILLED CLIMBER WILL SCALE THE TRUNK WITH THE AID OF A BELT MADE
FROM LIANAS AS HIS ONLY SUPPORT (209), IN ORDER TO REACH THE DRIPPING
GOLDEN COMBS (210). THE RISK, THEY CONSIDER, IS WORTH IT, FOR THESE NESTS
CAN YIELD 9KG/20LB OF HONEY DURING THE FOREST'S PEAK FLOWERING SEASON.

211

211 BAKA WOMEN IN PLANTATION, CAMEROON
(Lisa Silcock/Dja River Films)
ALTHOUGH THEY WERE ORIGINALLY COMPLETELY NOMADIC HUNTERS AND GATHERERS, IT IS PROBABLY SEVERAL CENTURIES SINCE THE BAKA BECAME SEMI-SETTLED AND BEGAN TO SUPPLEMENT THEIR DIET WITH CULTIVATED FOODS. STARCHY FOODS ARE PARTICULARLY SCARCE IN THE FOREST, SO THE CARBOHYDRATE OFFERED BY PLANTAINS, MANIOC AND THE LIKE IS HIGHLY DESIRABLE. SUCH FOODS ARE OFTEN GIVEN TO THE BAKA BY NEIGHBOURING VILLAGERS IN EXCHANGE FOR A DAY'S WORK; HOWEVER, SOME BAKA GROUPS NOW HAVE THEIR OWN PLANTATIONS, WHICH GIVES THEM FAR GREATER INDEPENDENCE.

212 YANOMAMI IN PLANTATION, BRAZIL (Peter Frey/Survival International)
THE YANOMAMI HUNT AND GATHER FOREST PRODUCE BUT ARE ALSO EXCELLENT SMALL-SCALE AGRICULTURALISTS. THEY CLEAR SMALL 'GARDENS' IN THE FOREST WHICH THEY PLANT WITH A HUGE VARIETY OF CROPS, INCLUDING PLANTAINS, MANIOC, PEACH PALMS, PAPAYA TREES, SUGAR CANE AND MAIZE. THEY ALSO CULTIVATE NON-FOOD PLANTS SUCH AS COTTON, MEDICINAL AND MAGIC PLANTS, HUNTING POISONS, AND OTHERS WHICH ARE MADE INTO ROPE AND ARROWS. NO ATTEMPT IS MADE TO PREVENT THESE GARDENS FROM BECOMING OVERGROWN: THEY ARE QUICKLY RECOLONIZED BY SEEDS FROM SURROUNDING TREES AND HAVE NO HARMFUL IMPACT ON THE FOREST.

213 BAKA PREPARING ARROW POISON, CAMEROON (Lisa Silcock/Dja River Films) PEOPLE FROM RAINFORESTS ALL OVER THE WORLD USE PLANT POISONS IN HUNTING, OFTEN EXPLOITING THE VERY COMPOUNDS THE PLANT HAS EVOLVED TO PROTECT ITSELF FROM PREDATORS. THE BAKA USE THE CRUSHED SEEDS OF A STROPHANTHUS VINE MIXED WITH OTHER PLANTS TO TIP THEIR CROSSBOW ARROWS. THE VINE CONTAINS STROPHANTHINE, A POTENT CARDIAC POISON WHICH IS USED IN WESTERN MEDICINE IN THE TREATMENT OF HEART DISEASE.

213

214 PENAN HUNTER USING A BLOW GUN, BORNEO (C. & B. Leimbach/Robert Harding Picture Library) THE SKILL OF BLOW GUN HUNTERS IS WELL DOCUMENTED, BUT THE FORCE OF THE ARROW ALONE WOULD BE INEFFECTIVE ON ALL BUT THE SMALLEST PREY. HOWEVER, EVEN A SLIGHT PUNCTURE BY A POISON-TIPPED DART IS ENOUGH TO KILL A LARGE ANIMAL: MONKEYS IN PARTICULAR ARE HUNTED IN THIS WAY. THE POISON ENTERS THE BLOODSTREAM, ARRESTING HEART FUNCTION WITHIN JUST A FEW MINUTES.

214

215 INDIANS WITH MONKEYS, ECUADOR

(John Wright/Hutchison Library)
THE MIRACLE OF HUNTING POISONS IS THAT THEY ARE INEFFECTIVE WHEN TAKEN BY MOUTH, SO THE MEAT IS QUITE SAFE TO EAT. RAINFOREST-DWELLING PEOPLES HAVE ACCUMULATED THEIR IMPRESSIVE AND USEFUL KNOWLEDGE OF PLANT PROPERTIES OVER A VERY LONG TIME. THIS INFORMATION IS POTENTIALLY EXTREMELY VALUABLE, EVEN LUCRATIVE – WHICH SHOULD ENCOURAGE EVEN THE MOST MERCENARY OF GOVERNMENTS TO SEE THE RAINFORESTS AS A RESOURCE TO BE PROTECTED.

215

217

216 BAKA FAMILY SHARING GAME, CAMEROON

(Lisa Silcock/Dja River Films)
MEAT IS PRIZED AMONG ALL
HUNTER-GATHERERS, AND RANKS
IN IMPORTANCE FAR ABOVE
VEGETABLE FOODS. AS WELL AS
HUNTING WITH POISON-TIPPED
ARROWS AND CROSSBOWS, THE
BAKA USE LONG SPEARS AND ALSO
SET TRAPS, THOUGH THIS IS A
BORROWED TECHNIQUE. THEY ARE
EXTREMELY SKILLED TRACKERS
WHO CAN IDENTIFY AND HUNT
DOWN AN ANIMAL GUIDED ONLY
BY THE FAINTEST HOOFPRINT, THE
SLIGHTEST SOUND, OR THE
CRUSHED VEGETATION WHICH
INDICATES ITS PATH.

217 GRILLING YAMS, PAPUA NEW GUINEA (Jack Fields/ZEFA)
YAMS ARE THE MAIN WILD SOURCE
OF STARCH FOUND IN THE WILD:
THEY TASTE BETTER BUT REQUIRE
MUCH MORE EFFORT TO PROCURE
THAN CULTIVATED FOODS.

218 EDIBLE BEETLE LARVAE, CAMEROON

(Lisa Silcock/Dja River Films)
SURPRISINGLY, PROTEIN IS NOT
ALWAYS EASY TO COME BY IN THE
FOREST: AT CERTAIN TIMES OF
YEAR GAME IS SCARCE AND THE
NUMBERS OF FISH, CRABS AND
SHRIMPS DWINDLE. EDIBLE
CATERPILLARS AND BEETLE LARVAE
THEN PROVIDE AN ALTERNATIVE
WHICH MAY SEEM REPELLENT TO
US, BUT WHICH IS HIGHLY
NUTRITIOUS.

218

219

219 WOMAN WEARING
TRADITIONAL FACE PAINT, PAPUA
NEW GUINEA (Mike McCoy/OSF)

220 APPLYING FACE PAINT, PAPUA
NEW GUINEA (Maureen Mackenzie/
Robert Harding Picture Library)

220

221 CHILD IN RITUAL PAINT OF CLOSING CEREMONY, PAPUA NEW GUINEA (Maureen Mackenzie/Robert Harding Picture Library)

DECORATION IS USED BY PEOPLE EVERYWHERE, BUT THE PAPUA NEW GUINEANS ARE MASTERS OF THE ART. THESE INTRICATE PATTERNS, WHICH CONTAIN BOTH ELEMENTS OF SPIRITUAL BELIEF AND REFERENCES TO THE NATURAL WORLD, ARE NOT JUST FOR EFFECT BUT ARE HIGHLY RITUALIZED AND USED ACCORDING TO STRICT RULES. SUCH SKILLS AND TRADITIONS, LIKE THE EXTENSIVE BUT UNWRITTEN KNOWLEDGE HELD BY THE FOREST PEOPLE, ARE PASSED DOWN ORALLY AND BY EXAMPLE THROUGH THE GENERATIONS. HEREIN LIES THEIR VULNERABILITY: CULTURAL KNOWLEDGE CAN DISAPPEAR ALL TOO EASILY FROM THE WORLD WHEN UNRECORDED, PARTICULARLY WHEN HELD BY A DISREGARDED MINORITY. THOUSANDS AND THOUSANDS OF FOREST PEOPLE HAVE ALREADY LOST THEIR LANDS AND CULTURAL IDENTITY, AND WITH THEM MANY CENTURIES OF ACCUMULATED LEARNING. THE WELFARE OF SUCH PEOPLE SHOULD BE PROTECTED ON COMPASSIONATE GROUNDS ALONE, BUT ALSO FOR THE SAKE OF THE FUTURE: FOR THE PEOPLE OF THE RAINFOREST MAY HOLD THE KEY TO A DIFFERENT, AND BETTER, WORLD FOR US ALL.

CONCLUSION
FUTURE IN THE BALANCE
ROGER HAMMOND

For millions of years, the rainforests of the world have existed relatively undisturbed. Their myriad animals and plants have evolved in response to their environment and to each other and generations of traditional rainforest people have survived by learning to live with their environment.

During the last century another culture has entered the forest: a culture driven by a pernicious cycle of growth and expansion. Natural checks against over-exploitation have been confounded because those who are now consuming the products of the forest are not those who experience the immediate effects of its degradation. There are millions who do, however, and it is now understood that in the short term the disappearance of rainforests will threaten the lives of over one billion people, as their water resources dry up and their land turns to dust. Many of these people actually live in the forests themselves and are utterly dependent on them. In the longer term this destruction may change the world's climate and therefore the history of the planet.

Pressures on our remaining forests are intense and it would be foolish to expect that all remaining forest can be protected. When environmental organizations work with governments to establish national parks and protected areas, it is vital to take account of the economic forces which impel people and institutions to abuse forests.

In principle there is much that can be done to satisfy the need to generate income whilst protecting the rainforests. Farmers can be taught new and more productive ways of using land and, if population growth can be controlled, a stable forest system can be the result. Tropical plantations may be rationalized through agroforestry so that they are economically and ecologically appropriate. Combinations of species may be grown which will provide higher and more sustainable income levels. Forest management can be reformed to relate harvests of logs to tree growth and regeneration rates. The nature of the harvest can be diversified to take account of outputs other than timber through the development of extractive reserves. Reserves for genetic resources can be paid for through royalties on existing forest products.

Knowledge and capital are needed to help develop farming systems and systems of integrated land use, systems which will result in long term and sustainable income both for individuals and for governments in countries which still retain intact rainforest.

Today, as we enter the last decade of the twentieth century, we have reached a turning point; we can no longer use the excuse of ignorance. We can now make informed decisions about the load we choose to place on our environment: decisions which we know will have an impact for years to come. Are we content to experiment with the loss for all time of a million or more species? Are we satisfied with the prospect of our climate being changed through our apparently insatiable demand for energy? Early this century Albert Einstein asserted that God did not play dice with the universe. Now, at the end of that century, are we prepared to gamble with the earth?

CRACKED AND USELESS EARTH – THE RESULTS OF MINING IN A FORMER
RAINFOREST AREA, BRAZIL
(Steve Bowles)

FEMALE GREEN ANOLE ON
HELICONIA, COSTA RICA
(Michael & Patricia Fogden)

INDEX

FIRST PUBLISHED IN GREAT BRITAIN IN 1989 BY
BARRIE & JENKINS LTD

THIS EDITION PUBLISHED BY CRESSET PRESS
BY RANDOM CENTURY GROUP LTD, RANDOM CENTURY HOUSE,
20 VAUXHALL BRIDGE ROAD, LONDON SW1V 2SA

RANDOM CENTURY GROUP AUSTRALIA (PTY) LTD, 20 ALFRED STREET,
MILSONS POINT, SYDNEY, NEW SOUTH WALES, 2061, AUSTRALIA

RANDOM CENTURY GROUP NEW ZEALAND LTD, 9-11 ROTHWELL AVENUE,
ALBANY, AUCKLAND 10, NEW ZEALAND

RANDOM CENTURY GROUP SOUTH AFRICA (PTY) LTD, PO BOX 337,
BERGVLEI, 2021 SOUTH AFRICA

A CIP CATALOGUE RECORD FOR THIS BOOK IS
AVAILABLE FROM THE BRITISH LIBRARY.

ISBN 0 09 175421 6

CONCEIVED AND EDITED: ANNE FURNISS
DESIGNER: DAVID FORDHAM
ASSISTANT DESIGNER: CAROL McCLEEVE
PICTURE RESEARCH: HELEN GILKS
PRODUCTION: ROBERT K. CHRISTIE
TYPESET BY SX COMPOSING LTD, RAYLEIGH, ESSEX
COLOUR SEPARATION BY WANDLE GRAPHICS
PRINTED AND BOUND IN SINGAPORE